Power up your Vocabulary; Grades 4-7

Ideal for Standardized tests

by

Justin J

Power up your Vocabulary

Copyright Notice

All rights reserved.

Do not duplicate or redistribute in any form.

Power up your Vocabulary

Table of Content

Section A1: How to Use This Book 8

Section A2: List of Abbreviations 10

Section A3: Glossary 11

Section B: Unit 1, Lesson 1 - Nominalisers 12

Section B: Unit 1, Lesson 2 - Nominalisers - Study Skills 14

    Exercise 1: Word Puzzle 16

    Exercise 2: Matching 18

    Exercise 3: Word family table 19

Section B: Unit 2, Lesson 1 - Nouns with Latin and Greek Roots - Science 20

Section B: Unit 2, Lesson 2 - Nouns with Latin and Greek Roots – Numbers 23

    Exercise 1: Scales 25

    Exercise 2: Root Trees 26

    Exercise 3: Word Search 28

Section B: Unit 3, Lesson 1 - Compound Nouns - the Environment 29

Section B, Unit 3, Lesson 2 - New Compounds - Travel and Tourism 31

    Exercise 1: Compound Crossword 33

    Exercise 2: Multiple Choice - Compounds 34

    Exercise 3: Word String 35

Section B, Unit 4, Lesson 1 - Extreme Adjectives - the Arts 36

Section B, Unit 4, Lesson 2 - News Adjectives 38

    Exercise 1: Ladders 40

    Exercise 2: Cloze Test 41

    Exercise 3: Word Tiles 42

Section B, Unit 5, Lesson 1: Adjective Synonyms - Celebrities 43

Section B, Unit 5, Lesson 2 - Compound Adjectives - Personality and Appearance 45

    Exercise 1: Match Synonyms and Compounds to Find a Celebrity 47

    Exercise 2: Finding the Mistakes in a Passage 48

    Exercise 3: Improving your Writing 49

Section B, Unit 6, Lesson 1 - Adjectives - Antonyms 50

Power up your Vocabulary

Section B, Unit 6, Lesson 2 - Antonyms with Prefixes - Critical Thinking 52
    Exercise 1: Antonym Bingo 54
    Exercise 2: Multiple Choice 55
    Exercise 3: Find the Mistake 56

Section B, Unit 7, Lesson 1- Process Verbs and Collocations 57

Section B, Unit 7, Lesson 2 - New Collocations - Digital Business 59
    Exercise 1: Multiple Choice 61
    Exercise 2: Cloze Test 61
    Exercise 3: Verb Replacement 62

Section B, Unit 8, Lesson 1 - Reporting Verbs - Social Sciences 63

Section B, Unit 8, Lesson 2 - Verbs in Critical Thinking 65
    Exercise 1: Words in the Nest 67
    Exercise 2: Cloze Test 68
    Exercise 3: Crossword 69

Section B, Unit 9, Lesson 1 - Phrasal Verbs 70

Section B, Unit 9, Lesson 2 - Phrasal Verbs in Context 72
    Exercise 1: Memory Game 74
    Exercise 2: Matching Sentence Halves 75
    Exercise 3: Meanings in Context 76

Section B, Unit 10, Lesson 1 - Describing Trends 77

Section B, Unit 10, Lesson 2 - Adding Adverbs 79
    Exercise 1: Labelling Graphs and Charts 81
    Exercise 2: Cloze Test 82
    Exercise 3: Oral Presentation 83

Section B, Unit 11, Lesson 1 - Idiomatic Verbs, New Trends in Business 84

Section B, Unit 11, Lesson 2 - Adverbs of Frequency, Shopping 86
    Exercise 1: Word Puzzle 88
    Exercise 2: Sentence Substitution 88
    Exercise 3: Making Sentences 89

Section B, Unit 12, Lesson 1 - Comment adverbs, the USA 90

Power up your Vocabulary

Section B, Unit 12, Lesson 2 - Adverbs for Perspective and Cohesion 92
    Exercise 1: Sentence Completion 94
    Exercise 2: Word Families 94
    Exercise 3: Jumbled Syllables 95

Section C, Unit 13, Lesson 1 - Common Mistakes 96

Section C, Unit 13, Lesson 2 - Homonyms 98
    Exercise 1: Multiple Choice 100
    Exercise 2: Find the Mistakes 101
    Exercise 3: Anagrams 101

Section C, Unit 14, Review, Units 1-13 102

Section D, Unit 15, Lesson 1 - Maths Vocabulary 104

Section D, Unit 15, Lesson 2 - More Maths Vocabulary 106
    Exercise 1: Word Puzzle 108
    Exercise 2: Complete the Questions 109
    Exercise 3: Word Finder 109

Section D, Unit 16, Lesson 1 - Science Vocabulary 110

Section D, Unit 16, Lesson 2 - More Science Vocabulary 112
    Exercise 1: Spidergrams 114
    Exercise 2: Sentence Completion 115
    Exercise 3: Classification 116

Section D, Unit 17, Lesson 1 - IT Vocabulary 117

Section D, Unit 17, Lesson 2 - More IT Vocabulary 119
    Exercise 1: Dialogue 121
    Exercise 2: Find the IT Phrase 122
    Exercise 3: Word String 123

Section D, Unit 18, Lesson 1 - Environmental Science Vocabulary 124

Section D, Unit 18, Lesson 2 - More Environmental Science Vocabulary 126
    Exercise 1: Multiple Choice, definitions and Usage 128
    Exercise 2: Complete a Factsheet 129
    Exercise 3: Word Search 130

Power up your Vocabulary

Section D, Unit 19, Lesson 1 - Historical Vocabulary 131
Section D, Unit 19, Lesson 2 - Geographical Vocabulary 133
    Exercise 1: Timeline 135
    Exercise 2: Labelling Pictures 135
    Exercise 3: Correct the Mistakes 136
Section D, Unit 20, Lesson 1 - Economics Vocabulary 137
Section D, Unit 20, Lesson 2 - More Economics Vocabulary 139
    Exercise 1: Matching Definitions 141
    Exercise 2: Antonyms 141
    Exercise 3: Describing Graphs 142
Section D, Unit 21, Lesson 1 - Arts Vocabulary 143
Section D, Unit 21, Lesson 2 - Visual Arts Vocabulary 145
    Exercise 1: Sentence Completion 147
    Exercise 2: Anagrams 147
    Exercise 3: Crossword 148
Section D, Unit 22, Lesson 1 - Literary Vocabulary 149
Section D, Unit 22, Lesson 2 – Drama and Poetry Vocabulary 151
    Exercise 1: Word Search 153
    Exercise 2: Multiple Choice 154
    Exercise 3: Complete a Vocabulary Usage Table 155
Section D, Unit 23, Lesson 1 - Media Vocabulary 156
Section D, Unit 23, Lesson 2 - Crime and Law Vocabulary 158
    Exercise 1: Cloze Test 160
    Exercise 2: Matching Definitions 161
    Exercise 3: Matching Suffixes 162
Section D, Unit 24, Lesson 1 - Citizenship Vocabulary 163
Section D, Unit 24, Lesson 2 - Ethics and Beliefs 165
    Exercise 1: Correct the Mistakes 167
    Exercise 2: Independent Writing 167
    Exercise 3: Word Puzzle 168

Power up your Vocabulary

Section D, Unit 25, Lesson 1 - Sports Vocabulary 169

Section D, Unit 25, Lesson 2 - Places and Equipment in Sport.. 171

    Exercise 1: Cloze Test 173

    Exercise 2: Complete a Table.. 174

    Exercise 3: Match Suffixes, Compounds and Collocations 175

Section E, Part 1 - Review of the Book... 176

    Activity 1: Snakes and Ladders 176

    Activity 2: Alphabet Quiz 180

Section E, Part 2 - Answers to Exercises 181

Section E, Part 3: Alphabetical Word List 210

Additional Bonus Material..218

Power up your Vocabulary

Section A2: List of Abbreviations

adj.	adjective
adv.	adverb
cf.	compared with
con	conjunction
e.g.	for example
n	noun
n (c)	noun countable
n (u)	noun uncountable
(n) (I)	Noun countable or uncountable depending on usage
prep	preposition
v	verb
v (I)	Intransitive verb (can stand alone)
v (T)	Transitive verb (requires an object)

Power up your Vocabulary

Section A3: Glossary

Adverbials	Expressions or parts of a sentence which modify the action
Antonyms	Words with opposite meanings e.g. large/small
Collective noun	Words which identify a collection of people or things as a single unit e.g. team, herd, class
Collocations	Words which are often used together e.g. verb + noun e.g. drive a car, adjective + noun e.g. delicious food
Compound nouns	Noun + noun (usually naming words)
Context	The words or sentences before and after a key word
Homographs	Words with the same spelling but different meanings depending on the context e.g. racket (n) (I) used to hit a tennis ball racket (n) (u) a lot of noise
Homophones	Words which sound the same but have different spellings and different meanings e.g. ate (a meal) eight (a number)
Nominalisers	Nouns formed by adding a suffix to a verb or adjective e.g. <u>verb</u>　　　　　<u>noun</u> educate　　　　educa**tion**
Parts of speech	Types of words with different functions in a sentence e.g. verb, noun, adjective, adverb
Prefix	The beginning of a word which tells you part of the meaning e.g. **un**happy
Root	The source of a word e.g. **astro**naut (astro is Latin. It means space)
Suffix	The ending of a word which tells you part of the meaning e.g. Japan**ese**
Synonyms	words with the same or similar meanings e.g. large/big

Power up your Vocabulary

Section B: Unit 1, Lesson 1 - Nominalisers

What are Nominalisers?

Nominalisers are nouns formed by adding a suffix to a verb or adjective. A suffix is an ending of a word. Many (but not all) suffixes tell you the part of speech. This helps you understand new words when reading.
Common noun suffixes used in this unit ……**tion**……**sion**……**ment**……**ance**…… **ity**
Nominalisers can be countable or uncountable nouns. Some can be both. Always make notes.
(n) (c) countable noun
(n) (u) uncountable noun
(n) (I) countable or uncountable depending on the context

Note:
Not all nouns have a suffix.
Nominalisers are used a lot in academic writing.
Learning nominalisers will improve your writing.

Dissertation (n) (c) dis-er-**tey**-sh*uh*
A long essay describing original research.
Example: In most universities students have to complete a dissertation for their degree.

Application (n) (c) ap-li-**key**-sh*uh*
A request for permission to enter an institution such as a school or college;
Putting something into practice; Of practical use.
Example: Parents have to complete an application for their child's school.

Enrollment (n) (I) en-**rohl**-m*uh* nt
The act of joining an organization such as a school.
Example: Most schools have an enrollment day before the start of term.

Registration (n) (I) rej-*uh*-**strey**-sh*uh*
The act of making an official record of something.
Example: In my school we have registration at 9am so that teachers can keep a record of who has attended class.

Presentation (n) (c) prez-*uh* n-**tey**-sh*uh*
The act of showing or explaining something, for example, to your classmates.
Example: I am nervous about the presentation I have to give in my history class next week.

Power up your Vocabulary

Experiment (n) (c) ek-**sper**-*uh*-ment
A scientific test to find out what happens.
Example
I love doing experiments in Mr Johnson's chemistry classes.

Elimination (n) (I) ih-lim-*uh*-**ney**-sh*uh* n
The act of ending or ruling out something.
Example
Multiple choice tests can often be answered by a process of elimination.

Assignment (n) (I) *uh*-**sahyn**-m*uh* nt
A piece of work somebody is required to do. The marks usually count for your course grade.
Example
We have several assignments to do in our English literature class this term.

Comprehension (n) (u) kom-pri-**hen**-sh*uh* n
The ability to understand something.
Example
I hate the comprehension tests Ms Mathews gives us in her English classes because I cannot understand them.

Classification (n) (I) klas-*uh*-fi-**key**-sh*uh* n
The action of organizing things into categories.
Example
The periodic table is a classification of elements.

Power up your Vocabulary

Section B: Unit 1, Lesson 2 - Nominalisers - Study Skills

> ### Vocabulary in use
>
> Some noun suffixes tell you part of the meaning of a word. Noun suffixes nearly always have the same spelling and pronunciation. Learn the spellings used in this unit. This will help you with dictation, listening and writing tests.
>
> ……tion   ……sion   ……ment   ……ance   ……ity

Motivation (n) (u) moh-t*uh*-**vey**-sh*uh* n
The reason for doing something.
<u>Example</u>
To learn successfully it is important to have strong motivation to excel in studies.

Determination (n) (I) dih-tur-m*uh*-**ney**-sh*uh* n
The quality of trying hard to succeed at something.
<u>Example</u>
I find maths very difficult. It takes a lot of determination to master it.

Commitment (n) (I) k*uh*-**mit**-m*uh* nt
A promise to do something or behave in a particular way.
<u>Example</u>
I have made a commitment to my parents to spend less time on social media and more time studying at weekends.

Distraction (n) (I) dih-**strak**-sh*uh* n
Something which stops you from focusing on a task.
<u>Example</u>
Cell phones are a distraction, so a lot of teachers make students turn them off in class.

Flexibility (n) (u) **flek**-s*uh*-b*uh* l -i-tee
The quality of being able to switch tasks or methods of working quickly.
<u>Example</u>
Modern education is constantly changing and flexibility is essential for ambitious students.

Power up your Vocabulary

> ## Word families
>
> Nominalisers are derived from a verb or adjective. Therefore, they are always part of a word family. You will expand your vocabulary faster if you learn families of words together.
>
> **Example**
>
> Verb: *motivate*   Noun (u): *motivation (act)*
> Noun (c): *motivator (person or thing)*   Adj: *motivated*
> Adverb: *motivationally*
>
> It is important to note the part of speech when you learn a new word. This will help you use the right word form from the family in your sentences.

Tenacity (n) (u)
The quality of refusing to give up.
Example
The school basketball team showed great tenacity and won the game even though their opponents were taller.

Concentration (n) (u)
The act of focusing on a task at hand.
Example
My teachers are always telling me that I lack concentration and that is why my exam results are poor.

Expectation (n) (c)
The belief that something is likely to happen.
Example
Teachers and students should have high expectations of the results they can achieve.

Communication (n) (I)
The act of passing information or emotions to other people.
Example
My English teacher says that good writing is all about communication of ideas and feelings.

Credibility (n) (u)
The condition of something being true or easy to believe.
Example
When doing research for class projects it is important to think about the credibility of online sources.

Power up your Vocabulary

Section B Unit 1, Exercises

Exercise 1: Word Puzzle

In some countries, not all children get an education. Read the definitions below. Match the words from the word bank. Fill in the squares, one letter in each square in the crossword on the next page. Number 1 has been done for you. The shaded squares form the name of someone who fights for the right to education for every child. Who is she?

1. *A scientific test to find out what happens.*

2. The action of a teacher checking which students are present in a class

3. The condition of something being true or easy to believe.

4. An extended piece of writing based on original research.

5. A request for permission to enter an institution such as a school or college

6. A piece of work somebody is required to do. The marks usually count for your course grades.

7. The quality of refusing to give up.

8. A promise to do something or behave in a particular way.

9. The act of passing information or emotions to other people.

10. The process of understanding something.

11. The reason for doing something.

12. The process of organizing information into categories.

13. Something which stops you from focusing on a task.

14. The act of focusing on a task at hand.

Word Bank

communication	distraction	dissertation	*experiment*
assignment	concentration	registration	classification
enrollment	comprehension	commitment	credibility
application	motivation	tenacity	

Power up your Vocabulary

| 1 | e | x | p | e | r | i | m | e | n | t |

2
3
4
5
6
7
8
9
10
11
12

z

13
14

m __ __ __ __ __   __ __ __ __ __ __ z __ __

(Did you get that right? Cross check your answer with the answer key at the end of the book)

Power up your Vocabulary

Exercise 2: Matching

Complete the diagram with words from this unit ending with the suffixes shown. The first one has been done for you.

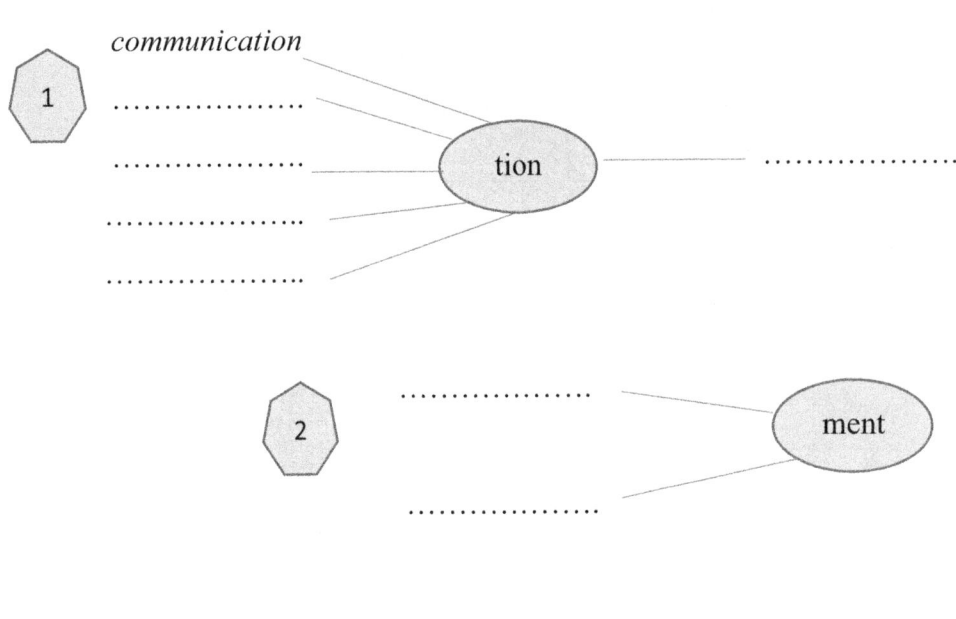

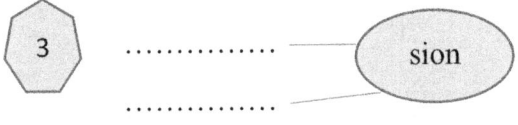

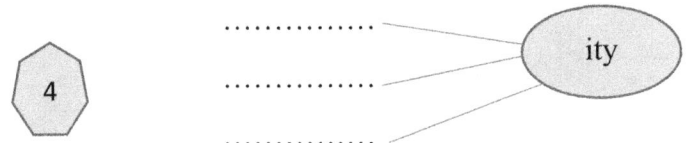

Power up your Vocabulary

Exercise 3: Word family table
Complete the table of word families. Number 1 has been done for you.

Study Tips

- Don't guess word families
- There are no simple rules for word forms or spellings
- Always use a dictionary and make notes
- Not all word families have all four parts of speech but there can be more than one noun
- The suffixes ...er, ...or and ...ant tell you the noun is a person. We will meet person suffixes again in **Unit 2**
- Don't invent words to fill in the blanks!

Verb	Noun	Adjective
permit	1. *permission*	permitted
2. _____	motivation motivator (person)	motivated
3. _____	presentation presenter (person)	xxxxxxxxxx
distract	4. _____	distracting
apply	5. _____ (object) applicant (person)	xxxxxxxxxx
experiment	experiment	6. _____
comprehend	7. _____	comprehensive
8. _____	satisfaction	9. _____
commit	commitment	10. _____

Power up your Vocabulary

Section B: Unit 2, Lesson 1 - Nouns with Latin and Greek Roots - Science

What are Roots?

The study of where words come from is called etymol**ogy**. A person who studies the origin of words is called an etymolog**ist**. Note the suffixes.

...ogy = an academic subject   ...ist = an expert in a subject

A lot of English words came from other languages. Etymologists study where these words came from; in other words, their roots or origins.

People who lived in the ancient Greek and Roman empires were interested in science. For a long-time other people didn't know much about science. But during the Renaissance (15th-16th century) they became interested in it. They read about science in ancient Greek and Latin books and borrowed the words.

When you understand Greek and Latin roots it will help you work out the meaning of many new words you will find in your science books.

Teachers call using roots and suffixes to understand new words, **decoding skills**.

Vocabulary in use

A root does not make a whole word in English. Many words also have a suffix. Some noun suffixes tell you part of the meaning of a word.

New noun suffixes in this unit:

.....**er** = person (male or female)   .... **ist** = person (male or female)

... **ism** = an idea or phenomenon   ... **ogy** = an academic subject

The same root can have more than one suffix. This is why there are sometimes two nouns in a word family as we saw in **Unit 1 Exercise 3**.

<u>Example</u>

Biology = academic subject

Biologist = a scientist who studies biology

It is important to use the correct word form.

Power up your Vocabulary

Cosmology (n) (u) koz-**mol**-*uh*-jee
Root: **cosm** = universe (Greek)
The study of the universe and its origins.
Example: Cosmology was used by ancient civilizations to explain the origins of the world.

Biomass (n) (u) **bahy**-oh-mas
Root: **bio** = life (Greek)
Material from living things such as straw and tree bark used as fuel to make energy.
Example: Some environmentalists believe that biomass can be used to generate electricity and reduce pollution.

Geology (n) (u) jee-**ol**-*uh*-jee
Root: **geo** = earth (Greek)
The study of the rocks which make up the earth.
Example: A knowledge of geology helps companies find resources such as oil and metals in the earth.

Gravity (n) (u) **grav**-i-tee
Root: **grav** = heavy (Latin)
The force which cause things to fall to the ground.
Example: The mathematician Isaac Newton developed the theory of gravity to explain why an apple fell on his head.

(the) **Lunar calendar** (n) (u) **loo**-ner **kal**-*uh* n-der
Root: **lun** = moon (Latin)
A calendar based on the movement of the moon around the earth.
Example: The date of some traditional holidays such as Easter and Chinese New Year are still based on the lunar calendar.

Orbit (n) (c) **awr**-bit
Root: **orb** = circle (Latin)
The regularly replicated route taken by an object e.g. a planet or a satellite around the earth.
Example: Google Maps relies on GPS (Global Positioning System) data from satellites travelling in orbit around the earth.

Physicist (n) (c) **fiz**-*uh*-sist
Root: **physi** = nature (Greek)
A person who studies natural phenomena such as light and sound.
Example: Stephen Hawking (1942-2018) was one of the most famous physicist in the world despite being disabled.

Power up your Vocabulary

Evaporation (n) (u) ih-vap-*uh*-**rey**-sh*uh* n
Root: **vap** = lack of (Latin)
The process of liquids turning to gas when heated.
Example: Global warming will probably increase the rate of evaporation from seas and lakes.

Solar power (n) (u) **soh**-ler pou-er
Root: **sol** = sun (Latin)
Electricity generated using the energy of the sun.
Example: Environmental groups urge governments to build more solar power stations instead of using coal or oil.

Electromagnetism (n) (u) ih-lek-troh-**mag**-ni-tiz-*uh* m
Root: **electra** = amber (Latin)
The phenomena associated with electric and magnetic fields and their interactions with each other.
Example: The principle of electromagnetism allows an electric car to run.

Vocabulary in use

Solar power and electromagnetism are compound nouns. Many other words formed from Latin and Greek roots are also compounds.

We will learn more about compound nouns in Unit 3.

Power up your Vocabulary

Section B: Unit 2, Lesson 2 - Nouns with Latin and Greek Roots – Numbers

> **Vocabulary in Use**
>
> We don't often use Roman numerals, (i ii iii iv v vi etc) any more. But Greek and Roman words for numbers are still used in hundreds of English words. They are very useful for maths and science but also help you understand new words in many other subjects as well.
>
> Numerical roots usually come at the beginning of an English word. Nouns formed with numerical roots are nearly always countable. Spellings can vary. Don't guess, use a dictionary. Numerical roots often appear in compound nouns. More on these in **Unit 3**.

Unilateral action (n) (c) yoo-n*uh*-**lat**-er-*uh* l ak-sh*uh* n
Root: **un/uni** = one (Latin)
An action taken by one party in negotiations or international affairs without the agreement of the other parties
Example: The United States took unilateral action by withdrawing from the Paris Climate Change Accord.

Monopoly (n) (c) m*uh*-**nop**-*uh*-lee
Root: **monos** = single, alone (Latin)
A market controlled by one company.
Example: Many countries have laws to stop businesses having a monopoly because monopolies usually raise prices.

Biplane (n) (c) **bahy**-pleyn
Root: **bi/bin/bis** = two (Latin)
An old type of aircraft with two pairs of wings, one above the other.
Example: Most of the aircraft used in WWI were biplanes.

Trigonometry (n) (u) trig-*uh*-**nom**-i-tree
Root: **tri** = three (Greek/Latin)
A branch of maths which studies sides and angles of a triangle.
Example: Trigonometry is essential to the science of map making.

Power up your Vocabulary

Quadrilateral (n) (c) kwod-r*uh*-**lat**-er-*uh* l
Root: **quadr** = four (Latin)
A shape in geometry with four sides.
Example: A quadrilateral with four equal sides is called a square.

Decade (n) (c) d*uh*-**keyd**
Root: **dec** = ten (Greek)
A period of ten years.
Example: The new airport will take a decade to build.

Centipede (n) (c) **sen**-t*uh*-peed
Root: **cent** = one hundred (Latin)
A creature with an elongated body composed of numerous segments each with a pair of legs.
Example: Biologists dispute whether centipedes should be classified as insects because they have more legs than flies or beetles.

Milligram (n) (c) **mil**-i-gram
Root: **mill** = thousand/one thousandth (Greek/Latin)
A unit for measuring weight used in chemistry, medicine and cooking (1000 milligrams (mg) = 1 gram)
Example: The doctor prescribed 5 milligrams of painkillers three times a day.

Multi-tasking (n) (u) **muhl**-tee-tasking
Root: **multi** = many (Latin)
The skill of being able to do several jobs at the same time.
Example: Multi-tasking is becoming more and more important in the modern workplace because of the spread of team working and digital technology.

Hemisphere (n) (c) **hem**-i-sfeer
Root: **hemi** = half (Greek)
Half of a sphere.
Example: Geographers, politicians and economists tend to divide the world into northern and southern hemispheres.

Power up your Vocabulary

Section B Unit 2, Exercises

Exercise 1: Scales

Complete the number scale below using roots in the correct order from the word bank. The first one has been done for you.

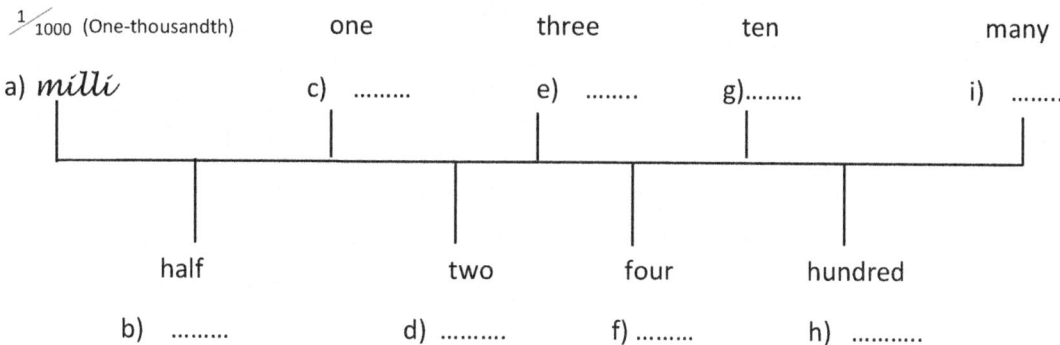

Word Bank		
tri	cent	mono
bi	multi	hemi
milli	quad	dec

Power up your Vocabulary

Exercise 2: Root Trees

Latin and Greek roots are used to form adjectives and verbs as well as nouns. Use the outlines below and the word bank to complete root trees. Remember roots can occur at the beginning, or in the middle of words and apply to any subject. Number 1 has been done for you as an example.

Word Bank

unification (n) (u) yoo-n*uh*-fi-**key**-sh*uh* n

centenary (n) (c) sen-**tee**-n*uh*-ree

decimate (v) **des**-*uh*-meyt

autobiography (n) (c) aw-t*uh*-bahy-**og**-r*uh*-fee

biodegradable (adj.) bahy-oh-di-**grey**-d*uh*-b*uh* l

universal (adj.)

decimal (adj.) **des**-*uh*-m*uh* l

centigrade (n) (c) **sen**-ti-greyd

unipolar (adj.) yoo-n*uh*-**poh**-ler

antibiotic (n) (c) an-ti-bahy-**ot**-ik

centurion (n) (c) sen-**too** r-ee-*uh* n

decathlon (n) (c) dih-**kath**-lon

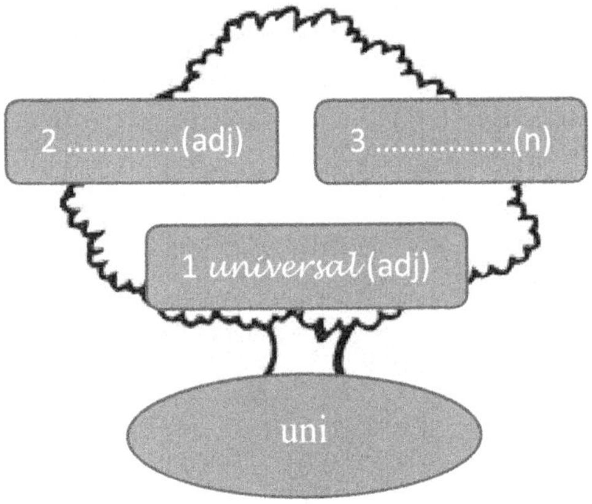

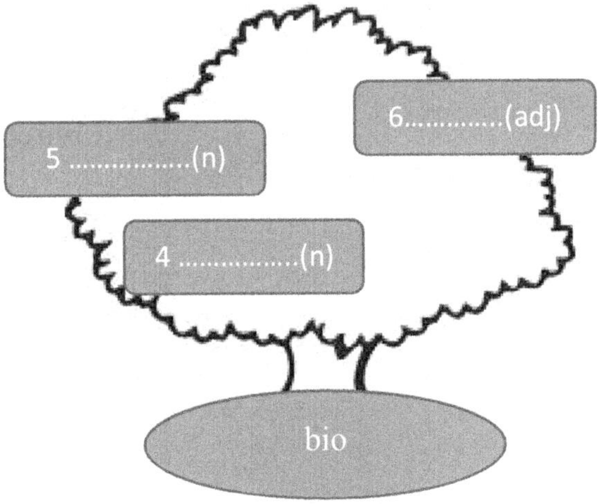

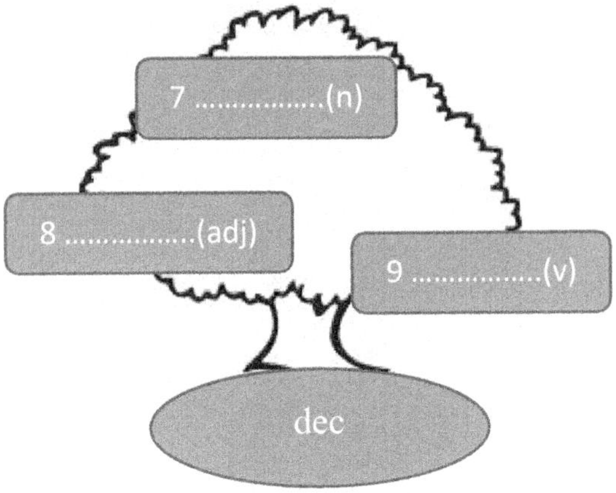

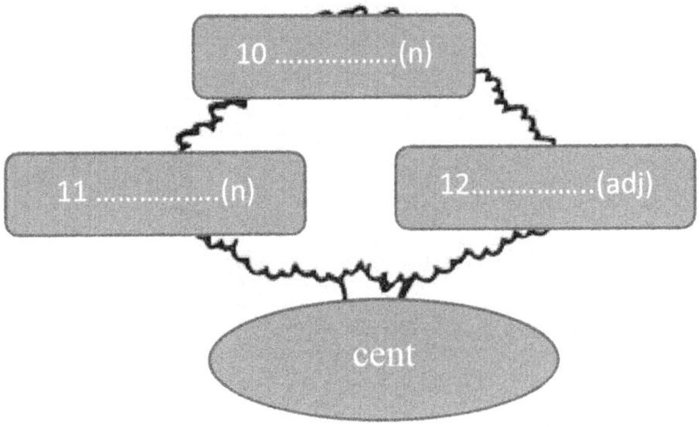

Tree 1 (root: **uni**)
- 1 *universal* (adj)
- 2 .... (adj)
- 3 .... (n)

Tree 2 (root: **bio**)
- 4 .... (n)
- 5 .... (n)
- 6 .... (adj)

Tree 3 (root: **dec**)
- 7 .... (n)
- 8 .... (adj)
- 9 .... (v)

Tree 4 (root: **cent**)
- 10 .... (n)
- 11 .... (n)
- 12 .... (adj)

Power up your Vocabulary

Now match the definitions to the numbers of the words in the root trees. There is more than one possible answer. Use the suffixes or a dictionary to help you if necessary. The first one has been done for you.

a)	*Something which occurs everywhere.*	1
b)	Material which breaks down and returns to nature over time e.g. leaves, paper.	-----
c)	The action of joining things into a single whole.	----
d)	A kind of medicine which works against infections.	----
e)	One hundred years after an important event.	----
f)	The story of person's life written by themselves.	----
g)	A Roman soldier who served in a unit of 100 men.	----
h)	A number system based on units of ten.	----
i)	A unit of measurement of temperature using a scale from 1 to 100 developed by the Swedish astronomer Anders Celsius.	----
j)	An athletic competition for men featuring ten events.	----
k)	A political world order dominated by one great power.	----
l)	To reduce something by one-tenth.	----

Power up your Vocabulary

Exercise 3: Word Search

Find the words below in the following puzzle. Words may be horizontal, vertical or diagonal and may be spelled forwards or backwards. The first one has been highlighted for you.

Nominalisers

```
Q D U O T S I C I S Y H P E G
H U Q C K P Y K T M N M G S R
K Y A W O C A L N I Y J D R A
G S L D H K E X O A G M U E V
E E S S R N T R M P A L Y V I
I U O J A I O I C N O K Z I T
M Q T L F G L C E F L N D N Y
E A P N O L Q A N N Q P O U X
R I R K I G W X T I B R O M D
B V M G F F Y D I E I W W E L
U Q R Q I T Z B G Z R G C H A
O A L G Q O H K R F T A C E T
M C N U I A U Z A D D A L D I
H G M H L S M K D E C I M A L
E L O O Y B N P E Z K F M V U
```

BIPLANE	CENTIGRADE	DECADE	DECIMAL
GEOLOGY	GRAVITY	MILLIGRAM	MONOPOLY
ORBIT	PHYSICIST	QUADRILATERAL	UNIVERSE

Take it Further

For the history of the English language including the introduction of Greek and Latin roots see:
http://www.bbc.co.uk/history/british/lang_gallery.shtml

For the famous scientists mentioned in the definitions in this unit see:
Anders Celsius: https://www.biography.com/people/anders-celsius-9242754
Stephen Hawking: https://www.space.com/15923-stephen-hawking.html
Isaac Newton: https://www.ducksters.com/biography/scientists/isaac_newton.php

Power up your Vocabulary

Section B: Unit 3, Lesson 1 - Compound Nouns - the Environment

> **What are compound nouns?**
> In this unit we will learn about a third way of forming nouns. Compound nouns are formed by putting two nouns together. They are usually countable unless they name a process, a liquid or a force. In most cases, only the first word of the compound is capitalised. In this lesson we will look at some compound nouns relating to the environment, first some words to describe problems, then some words to describe solutions.
>
> Examples from Units 1 and 2: nominalisers and roots
> 1. application + form = application form (n) (c)
>   A piece of paper or website page which you have to fill in to apply for something.
> 2. solar + system = solar system (n) (c)
>   All the planets which orbit around a sun.

(the) Ozone layer (n) (u) **oh**-zohn **ley**-er
A level in the upper atmosphere where the gas, ozone, is concentrated.
Example
Emissions of gases called CFCs caused a large hole to appear in the Ozone Layer in the 1980s.

Greenhouse gas (n) (c) **green**-hous gas
A group of gases (e.g. carbon dioxide, methane) which when released into the atmosphere contribute to climate change.
Example
International agreements now require countries to emit less greenhouse gases.

Soil erosion (n) (u) soil ih-**roh**-zh*uh* n
The process of soil being lost due to the action of wind or rain.
Example
Soil erosion means that farmers can grow less food which reduces their incomes.

Ocean current (n) (c) **oh**-sh*uh* n **kur**-*uh* nt
The movement of a body of hot or cold water in the sea travelling in a particular direction.
Example
Some scientists fear that climate change may cause ocean currents to change direction.

Acid rain (n) (u) **as**-id reyn
Rain which has been contaminated with acid from chemicals in the atmosphere.
Example
When acid rain falls on a city it can cause corrosion in cars and buildings.

Power up your Vocabulary

Vocabulary in Use 1

The same base word can have many compounds with different meanings. Learning multiple compounds formed with the same base word makes your academic vocabulary more precise.

Carbon capture (n) (u) **kahr**-b*uh* n **kap**-cher
The process of preventing gases such as CO2 (Carbon dioxide) from escaping into the atmosphere.
Example
Carbon capture can be used to reduce emissions from power stations. The captured gas is buried.

Carbon footprint (n) (c) **kahr**-b*uh* n **foo** t-print
A measure of the total amount of gases containing carbon produced by a building or process.
Example
Modern architects are trying to reduce the carbon footprint of their buildings by using environmentally friendly materials.

Carbon trading (n) (u) **kahr**-b*uh* n treyd-ing
The practice of companies or countries buying and selling licences to produce gases containing carbon.
Example
Some companies say they cannot meet targets to reduce their carbon emissions, so they use carbon trading markets to buy additional licences to get around the law.

Vocabulary in Use 2

Some compound nouns are formed by putting an adjective in front of the base noun.

Catalytic converter (n) (c) k*uh*-**tal**-*uh*-tik k*uh* n-**vur**-ter
A device fitted to cars which changes exhaust gases from car engines into less dangerous substances.
Example
Most modern cars are fitted with a catalytic converter to protect the environment.

Renewable energy (n) (u) ri-**noo-ey**-b*uh* l **en**-er-jee
All naturally occurring sources of energy which do not run out e.g. **biomass** and **solar power**.
Example
Most countries are developing sources of renewable energy to replace coal or oil-fired power stations.

Power up your Vocabulary

Section B, Unit 3, Lesson 2 - New Compounds - Travel and Tourism

Vocabulary in Use

English has become the dominant world language in the 21st century. One important reason for this is that English has the ability to form new words to describe new technology. The main way English creates new words is by using roots and compounds.

The way we travel is changing very quickly in response to the environmental issues we studied in Lesson 1. Now we will learn some compound nouns for the latest in travel and transport.

Hybrid car (n) (c) **hahy**-brid kahr
A car which uses both gas and electricity to run.
Example
Nissan is one of the largest manufacturer of hybrid cars in the world.

Hydrogen fuel cell (n) (c) **hahy**-dr*uh*-j*uh* n **fyoo**-*uh* l sel
A device which produces an electric current to power a car from the oxidation of hydrogen.
Example
Some car manufacturers believe that hydrogen fuel cells are a cleaner alternative to gas engines than hybrid or battery powered cars.

Driverless car (n) (c) **drahy**-ver-lis kahr
A car which is controlled by a computer instead of a human driver.
Example
A lot of companies including Apple and Google are testing driverless cars but there are still a lot of technical challenges.

Charging station (n) (c) chahrj-ing **stey**-sh*uh* n
A place, similar to a gas station, where drivers can recharge the batteries of electric cars.
Example
There are not enough charging stations yet, so some people will not buy electric cars.

Eco-tourism (n) (u) **ee**-koh **too** r-iz-*uh* m
A form of tourism which tries to minimise the impact of the traveller on the environment.
Example
Experts say that eco-tourism is essential to protect unspoilt areas such as Antarctica.

Power up your Vocabulary

Vocabulary in Use

Compound nouns can be tricky to use correctly. The base word is not always the first word of a compound. Compounds can be formed by putting another noun or adjective in front of the base word. Some compounds also have more than two words e.g. hydorgen fuel cell.

- Some compound nouns are one word (closed form compounds) e.g. **airport**
- Some compound nouns are two or more words with a space between them (open form compounds) e.g. **pedestrian zone**.
- Some compound nouns are hyphenated e.g. **mono-rail**

There are no simple rules. Do not guess, use a dictionary.

Long-haul flight (n) (c) lawng hawl flahyt
A flight which covers a long distance.
Example
The growing number of long haul flights emit dangerous levels of pollution at high altitudes.

Budget airline (n) (c) **buhj**-it **air**-lahyn
An airline which sells cheap tickets but offers few services.
Example
Budget airlines have made overseas travel possible for a lot more people in the last 20-30 years.

Monorail (n) (I)
A kind of train which runs on a single track often suspended above the ground.
Example
Manchester has one of the most advanced monorail systems in the world.

Pedestrian Zone (n) (c) p*uh*-**des**-tree-*uh* n zohn
An area of a city where vehicles are not allowed to enter.
Example
Planners argue that pedestrian zones mean cleaner air for shoppers.

Ride-sharing app (n) (c) **rahyd**-shair-ing ap
An internet-based service where people can arrange to share one car instead of each using their own car.
Example
If ride sharing apps become popular, it may mean fewer cars on the roads.

Section B, Unit 3, Exercises

Exercise 1: Compound Crossword

Note: There are no spaces between parts of each compound in this puzzle.

Across
5. A car powered by gas and electric engines
6. A company offering cheap flights
7. A measure of the pollution emitted by a building
8. Power from sources which will never run out

Down
1. A level of the atmosphere
2. Loss of earth due to wind and rain
3. A place to recharge electric cars
4. Travel which does not harm the environment

Power up your Vocabulary

Exercise 2: Multiple Choice - Compounds

Choose the best answer for each of the following questions:

Example
(b) Which of the following compounds describes a means of getting a taxi using your cell phone:
   a) charging station   b) ride sharing app   c) pedestrian zone
   d) catalytic converter

1. (   ) Which of the following compounds describes a car controlled by a computer:

   a) e mobility   b) hybrid car   c) hydrogen fuel cell   d) driverless car

2. (   ) Which of the following compounds is correctly punctuated:

   a) longhaulflight   b) long haul flight   c) long-haul flight   d) long haul-flight

3. (   ) Which of the following is <u>not</u> a compound word of carbon:

   a) carbon trading   b) carbon net   c) carbon footprint   d) carbon capture

4. (   ) Which of the following sentences is the best definition of a charging station:

   a) A place where drivers can top up their cell phones.

   b) A place where you can catch a bus or train.

   c) A place where drivers can fill up their cars with gas.

   d) A place where drivers can charge the batteries of their electric cars.

5. (   ) Which of the following compounds completes the sentence; Some scientists fear that climate change could cause the ……………………….. to flow in the opposite direction:

   a) ocean currents   b) soil erosion   c) acid rain   d) catalytic converter

6. (   ) Which of the following means an urban transport system using one rail:

   a) uni rail   b) mono rail   c) mono track   d) geo railway

Power up your Vocabulary

Exercise 3: Word String

How many compound nouns can you find in this? The first one has been highlighted for you. Write them below.

Pedestrianzonegreenhousegashybridcarhydrogenfuelcellcarbontradingoceancurrentozonelayerecotourismsoilerosion

Pedestrian zone ....

....

Power up your Vocabulary

Section B, Unit 4, Lesson 1 - Extreme Adjectives - the Arts

What are Extreme Adjectives?

We often say things like, "This painting is **very good**." Extreme adjectives replace **very .....** with a single word, for example "This painting is **brilliant**." Extreme adjectives are at the top or bottom of a scale or ladder. For example we can review a movie and say that the movie is ---------------------→

su...
go...
av...
poor
appalling

Extreme adjectives are descriptive and so are widely used in novels, news reports and advertising. There is often more than one adjective which is a synonym for *very something*. The more you know the better.

Tragic (adj.) **traj**-ik
very sad
Example
Hamlet by William Shakespeare is the tragic story of the prince of Denmark who has to reconcile his desire for oblivion with his duty to avenge his father's murder.

Breath-taking (adj) **breth**-tey-king
very exciting, impressive or beautiful
Example
The cinematography in the film "Blade Runner" is breath-taking.

Absurd (adj.) ab-**surd**
very silly, stupid, illogical or untrue
Example
The plot in Smith's latest novel is absurd. I do not recommend his book.

Terrifying (adj.) **ter**-*uh*-fahy-ing
very frightening, scary
Example
The special effects in some horror movies are terrifying.

Formidable (adj.) **fawr**-mi-d*uh*-b*uh*l
very strong, impressive, powerful or worthy of respect
Example
Brad Pitt showed his formidable talent in a supporting role in the film Thelma and Louise.

Power up your Vocabulary

Vocabulary in Use

Adverbs can be used to modify adjectives or make them more precise. There are special rules about which adverbs can, and cannot, be used to modify extreme adjectives.

~~Tonight's episode of the soap opera is very awful.~~

Tonight's episode of the soap opera is really awful.

Tonight's episode of the soap opera is absolutely awful.

Hilarious (adj.) hi-**lair**-ee-*uh* s
very funny
Example
My dad thinks the first series of the TV comedy Dad's Army were hilarious.

Scintillating (adj.) **sin**-tl-ey-ting
very clever, amusing, interesting
Example
The latest exhibition at the city gallery includes some scintillating work by local artists.

Furious (adj.) **fyoo** r-ee-*uh* s
very angry
Example
The demolition of another historic building has provoked a furious reaction from historians.

Stupendous (adj.) stoo-**pen**-d*uh* s
very large or impressive, better than expected
Example
The paintings on the ceiling of the Sistine Chapel in Rome were a stupendous achievement by Michelangelo.

Inspired (adj.) in-**spahy***uh* rd
very original, innovative but based on instinct or feelings rather than knowledge
Example
Disney made an inspired decision to make Toy Story entirely by computer animation.

Power up your Vocabulary

Section B, Unit 4, Lesson 2 - News Adjectives

> ## Vocabulary in Use
>
> A lot of extreme adjectives have ….ing and ……ed forms. Remember:
>
> ……. ing describes an object.   …… ed describes a state of mind
>
> Compare: a) The Prime minister was appalled by General Ali's remarks.
>   b) The Prime Minister said that General Ali's remarks were appalling.
>
> Make sure you use the correct form in your sentences.
>
> News reports often use adjective synonyms shown in pairs below.

Disgusting/disgusted (adj.) dis-**guhs**-ting   dis-**guhstid**
Appalling/appalled (adj.) *uh*-**paw**-ling   *uh*-**pawld**
very unpleasant, unacceptable, shocking
Example
A new report says conditions in some of the country's prisons are absolutely disgusting.   Human rights campaigners said they were appalled.

Astonishing/astonished (adj.)   *uh*-**ston**-ish-ing   *uh*-**ston**-isht
Amazing/amazed (adj.) *uh*-**mey**-zing   *uh*-**meyzd**
very surprised/surprising
Example
The government has announced astonishing changes to the tax system. The opposition leader said she was amazed.

Mesmerizing/mesmerized mez-m*uh*-rahyzing   mez-m*uh*-rahyzd
Thrilling/thrilled (adj.) **thril**-ing   thrild
very exciting/excited. Describing something you could not take your eyes off.
Example
Manchester United produced a mesmerizing performance to win the Champions League final last night. Fans watching in pubs around the country were thrilled.

Power up your Vocabulary

> ## Vocabulary in Use
>
> Not all extreme adjectives have **...ing** or **...ed** endings. Some have suffixes. We have already met suffixes used to form a noun from a verb. Now we will meet suffixes used on their own to indicate an adjective or to form an adjective from a noun or verb. In some cases, there are word families you should learn.
>
> Suffixes introduced in this unit:
>
> ic   ..... ous   ..... ful   ...... less
>
> These endings tell you that a word is an adjective and can help you guess the meaning of new vocabulary in reading.

spotless (adj.) **spot**-lis
very clean
Example
The troops wore spotless uniforms for the annual military parade.

Outrageous (adj.) out-**rey**-j*uh* s   noun: outrage   verb: outrage   adverb: outrageously
Very shocking and unacceptable behavior.
Example
World leaders condemned todays terrorist attack as outrageous.

Iconic (adj.) ahy-**kon**-ik   noun: icon
Acting as a sign or symbol of something, usually a culture or tradition.
Example
The Forbidden City is an iconic symbol of Beijing and ancient Chinese culture.

Dreadful (adj.) **dred**-f*uh* l   noun: dread   verb: dread   adverb: dreadfully
Very bad or unpleasant, causing fear. Often used before a noun to emphasize how bad a situation is.
Example
The Foreign Secretary offered his sympathies to the families of victims of the dreadful earthquake in Iran.

Section B, Unit 4, Exercises

Exercise 1: Ladders

In the contexts given below which extreme adjective from this Unit belongs at the top or bottom of the ladder? There is more than one possible answer in some cases. The first one has been done for you.

a) a TV comedy

a *hilarious*

a funny

b) a travel brochure

....

...utiful

c) a criminal court

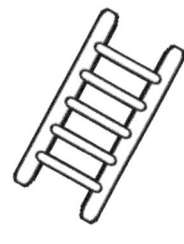

bad behav...

.... behavior

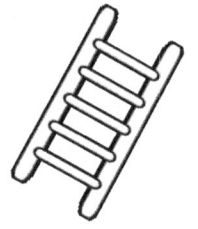

d) news of a scientific breakthrough

a .... achiev...

an important achie...

e) a news report of something unexpected

an .... ev...

an unusual event

f) a play with an unhappy ending

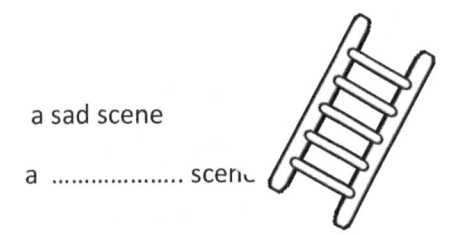

a sad scene

a .... scene

g) a historic building

an ....

a famous s...

Power up your Vocabulary

Exercise 2: Cloze Test

Read the following movie reviews from an entertainment guide. Fill in the blanks with the most appropriate extreme adjective from the word bank. Use context clues in the text to help you. Each word can only be used once. Number 1 has been done for you as an example.

After the Oscar winning success of his last movie I expected a lot from the latest offering from Shay Williams but I have to say *The 21st Century Vampire* is disappointing. There are some good points. Some of the 3D special effects are (1) *terrifying* and Clara Chambers gives a (2) …………………. debut performance as the secretary kidnapped by a robot turned vampire. But even she cannot carry a plot that is frankly (3) ………………….. and the rest of the cast, also mostly unknowns, should go back to drama school. They were so (4) ………………………. that the mood created by the special effects was broken and what is meant to be a horror film actually had the audience laughing. One scene in particular where the boss, who is secretly in love with his kidnapped secretary, tries to hack into the robot's software to make him release her is just (5) ………………………… I should give this one a miss if I were you.

On the other hand, Jason Timberlake's topical adaptation of Chaucer's Canterbury Tales is (6) …………………. The plot is emotive and original with some (7) ……………………… twists and turns that kept me on the edge of my seat for the whole two hours. There are no big-name stars but that doesn't matter; the movie is all about how the group of pilgrims from Africa interact on their journey to the shrine of Europe and it works. Some of the cinematography is (8) ……………………….. . The pilgrim's hopes are repeatedly thwarted by some (9) ……………………… behavior from people smugglers and bureaucrats alike. The pilgrims time and again recover from setbacks, showing great tenacity. The movie is partly about the strength of the human spirit but their journey finally ends in disaster. Ultimately this is a (10) …………… film but one that you have to see.

Word Bank

breath taking	awful	stupendous
inspired	amazing	*terrifying*
hilarious	tragic	absurd
outrageous		

Power up your Vocabulary

Exercise 3: Word Tiles

Match a tile in column A with a tile in column B to make an extreme adjective. Write the answers in the spaces below. The first one has been done for you.

A

1. disgus
3. formid
5. mesmer
7. dread
9. thril
11. appall
13. icon
15. stupen
17. hilar
19. breath

B

2. ful
4. ed
6. ting
8. ic
10. dous
12. able
14. taking
16. ling
18. ized
20. ious

Answers

i) (1 + 6) *disgusting*   ii) (3 +) ……………   iii) (5 +) ……………   iv) (7 +) ……………

v) (9 +) ……………   vi) (11 +) ……………   vii) (13 +) ……………   viii) (15 +) ……………

ix) (17 +) ……………   x) (19 +) ……………

Power up your Vocabulary

Section B, Unit 5, Lesson 1: Adjective Synonyms - Celebrities

> **What are synonyms?**
>
> Synonyms are words or phrases with the same or similar meanings. Synonyms are nearly always the same part of speech. In other words, a synonym for an adjective is another adjective not a noun or verb.
>
> Some students use the same common words all the time. But ambitious students learn synonyms for common words, especially adjectives. Using a good range of synonyms makes your oral presentations and writing less repetitive and more interesting. This will raise your scores in **assignments** and tests.
>
> Modern culture is fascinated by celebrities, so in this unit we will learn synonyms for celebrities, their personalities and lifestyles.

Common word: famous   Synonym: **renowned** (adj.) ri-**nound**
Example
J.K. Rowling is the renowned author of the Harry Potter books.

Common word: rich   Synonym: **wealthy** (adj.) **wel**-thee
Example
Motor racing has made Lewis Hamilton a very wealthy man.

Common word: beautiful   Synonym: **glamorous** (adj.) **glam**-er-*uh* s
Example
Elizabeth Taylor was one of the most glamorous film stars of the 20th century.

Common word: desk-bound   Synonym: **sedentary** (adj.) **sed**-n-ter-ee
Example
A sedentary lifestyle is bad for health.

Common word: clever   Synonym: **astute** (adj.) *uh*-**stoot**
Example
Steve Jobs became a Silicon Valley celebrity partly because he was an astute businessman.

Vocabulary in Use: Register

Register is about the formality of language. Both nouns and adjectives can be <u>informal</u> or <u>formal</u>. Informal expressions, sometimes called slang, are used in everyday speech. Formal expressions are found in text books and used in academic writing. There are often nouns and adjectives which have the same meaning, so are synonyms, but have different registers. If you want to improve your English quickly then get in the habit of making notes of register when learning new words.

<u>Example</u>   Formal adjective: **wealthy** (adj.)   Informal adjective: loaded (adj.)

In this lesson we will learn some formal adjectives to describe the personality of celebrities. Note that many of these words use the adjective suffixes we met in unit 4.

Extrovert (adj.) **ek**-str*uh*-vurt   informal: lively
Describing someone who is confident and enjoys being with other people.
<u>Example</u>
Most celebrities are extrovert personalities who enjoy making public appearances.

Photogenic (adj.) foh-t*uh*-**jen**-ik   informal: attractive
Describing someone who looks good in photographs or on TV.
<u>Example</u>
Princess Diana was the most photogenic member of the Royal Family and was followed everywhere by photographers.

Charismatic (adj.) kar-iz-**mat**-ik   Informal: zippy
Describing someone who has a powerful, personal quality that impresses and influences others.
<u>Example</u>
Companies look for charismatic personalities to appear in their advertisements.

Notorious (adj.) noh-**tawr**-ee-*uh*s   Informal: bad ass
Describing someone who is famous for being bad or behaving in **appalling** ways.
<u>Example</u>
Justin Bieber and Lady Gaga are two notorious celebrities.

Cosmopolitan (adj.) koz-m*uh*-**pol**-i-tn   Informal: global
Describing someone who lives a sophisticated, international lifestyle, usually in modern cities.
<u>Example</u>
A lot of celebrities live in cosmopolitan cities such as London, Paris and New York.

Power up your Vocabulary

Section B, Unit 5, Lesson 2 - Compound Adjectives - Personality and Appearance

> **What are compound adjectives?**
>
> In Unit 3 we saw how two nouns can be used together to create a compound. Two adjectives can be used in the same way. The resulting compound adjectives are usually hyphenated.
>
> Compound adjectives are usually semi- formal and idiomatic in register. This makes them very useful in speaking tests, interviews and presentations.
>
> In this lesson we will learn some compound adjectives to describe personality and appearance.

Level-headed (adj.) **lev**-*uh* l-**hed**-id
Describes someone who has a lot of common sense, stays calm and can make good decisions under pressure.
Example
Gareth Southgate, the England football manager, has a very level-headed approach to the game.

Light-hearted (adj.) **lahyt**-**hahr**-tid
Describes someone who likes to laugh a lot and rarely gets worried.
Example
Well known comedians such as Billy Connolly are often light-hearted people.

Absent-minded (adj.) **ab**-s*uh* nt-**mahyn**-did
Describes somebody who is often lost in deep thought and tends to forget simple, everyday things.
Example
It is a popular myth that great scientists like Einstein are always absent minded.

Big-headed (adj.) **big**-hed-id
Describes someone who is selfish and believes that they are more important than they really are.
Example
Some people think that a lot of celebrities are big headed and have not really done anything important.

Two-faced (adj.) **too**-feyst
Describes someone who says one thing and does another.
Example
Politicians who promise to cut taxes and then raise them are said to be two-faced.

Power up your Vocabulary

> **Vocabulary in Use:**
>
> When describing celebrity, wealth and personal appearance be careful about politeness. For example, it is often rude to call a person fat. Idiomatic synonyms such as chubby, plump or curvy are often less direct and less offensive. Some compound adjectives can have the same role; to soften the impact of what we are saying.

Well-heeled (adj.) **wel-heeld**
A less direct way of saying that somebody is rich.
Example
The CEOs of Fortune 500 companies are usually well-heeled but often do not like being called rich.

Well-groomed (adj.) **wel-groomd**
Describes somebody who is always smart and well dressed.
Example
Companies expect celebrities who are paid to be corporate ambassadors to be well-groomed.

Mass-produced (adj.) **mas-pr*uh*-doosd**
Describes products which are produced in large quantities and every item is the same. Sometimes used as a less direct way of saying cheap.
Example
Most celebrities avoid being photographed in mass-produced clothes because it cheapens their image.

Designer label (adj.) **dih-zahy-ner-ley-b***uh*
Describes products produced in small quantities or by hand which are expensive and exclusive.
Example
French companies produce many of the most desirable designer label brands including clothes, handbags and make up often worn by A-list celebrities.

Far-fetched (adj.) **fahr-fecht**
Describes a story or news report which lacks **credibility**. Sometimes used as a less direct way of saying that something is lies or nonsense.
Example
The latest stories in the media about the rock star's marriage seem rather far-fetched.

Section B, Unit 5, Exercises

Exercise 1: Match Synonyms and Compounds to Find a Celebrity

Match a word from box A with a word from box B to make a pair of synonyms or a compound adjective. The first one has been done for you.

	A	
i clever	ii famous	
iii lively	iv rich	
v mass	vi well	
vii desk-bound	viii	
designer		

	B	
label	wealthy	
sedentary	produced	
hearted	fetched	
extrovert	astute	
renowned	groomed	

i) clever = astute ii) .... iii) ....
iv) .... v) .... vi) ....
vii) .... viii) .... ix) ....
x) ....

Now complete the name of a world-famous singer with letters from your answer.

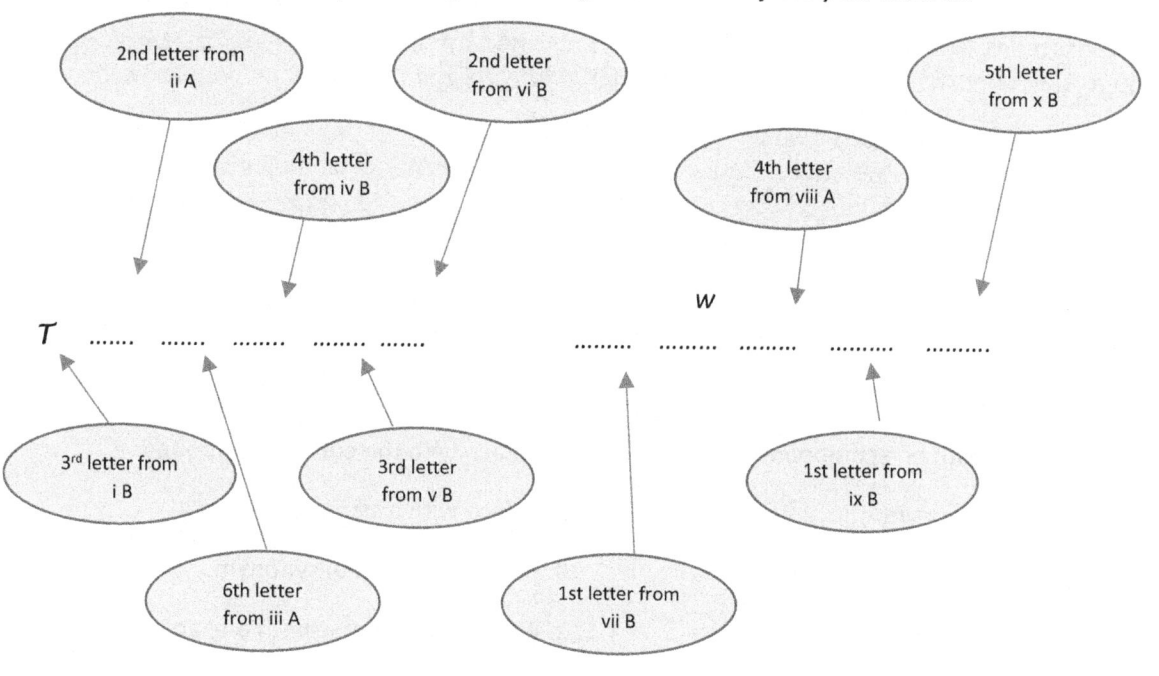

T ....

Clues:
- 2nd letter from ii A
- 4th letter from iv B
- 2nd letter from vi B
- 4th letter from viii A
- 5th letter from x B
- 3rd letter from i B
- 6th letter from iii A
- 3rd letter from v B
- 1st letter from vii B
- 1st letter from ix B

w

Power up your Vocabulary

Exercise 2: Finding the Mistakes in a Passage

Correct the highlighted passages in the text below using vocabulary from Units 4 and 5. The first one has been done for you.

A Celebrity Couple I Admire

it is a bit tough for me to pick a celebrity couple to write about as there are so many to choose from. but finally, I have decided to write about David and Victoria Beckham.

David Beckham was born in Leytonstone, London in 1975 and still lives there with his wife, Victoria, and their four children. David Beckham is best known as a footballer who played for England from 1996 to 2009 and also for (1) ~~icon~~ *iconic* clubs like Manchester United and Real Madrid. As a professional player, he became a legend around the world, particularly for his bending free kicks and (2) refusal to ever give up in matches.

Thanks to his skill and personality Beckham became one of the highest earners in footballer and, although he has now retired, he remains a very (3) rich man. After playing in Britain, Spain and the USA he also enjoys a (4) global lifestyle. But he has tried to give something back to society as a UNICEF ambassador and through the "David Beckham UNICEF Fund" to help protect children around the world. If fact, one of the keys to Beckham's success is that, despite his fame, he has never become (5) selfish person and never thought he was more important than the team. He has established a second career as a model and spokesperson who is always (6) well-heeled and a (7) clever businessman. Despite some appalling stories published by certain (8) famous for being bad newspapers David Beckham has always been (9) straight-headed and remains as popular as ever.

Meanwhile, Victoria Beckham has also continued her singing career and has become (10) famous as a fashion entrepreneur as well marketing a range of (11) designerlabel clothes and accessories worldwide. Despite being a mother of four, she is still one of the most (12) attractive to a photographer women in the world. I wish them all the best for the future.

1. *Replace with correct word form.*

2. Replace with a strong adjective from Unit 4.

3. Use a more formal synonym.

4. Use a more formal synonym.

5. Replace this phrase with one compound adjective.

6. Replace with the correct compound.

7. Use a more formal synonym.

8. Replace with a strong adjective.

9. Use the correct compound.

10. Use a more formal synonym.

11. Correct the punctuation.

12. Replace this phrase with one adjective.

Power up your Vocabulary

Exercise 3: Improving your Writing

Write a short essay (250-300 words) about a celebrity of your choice. Describe their personality, life style and appearance. Try to use at least five of the new words you have learned in this unit.

> ### Take it Further
>
> Find out more about the celebrity in the word puzzle (Exercise 1)
>
> Her biography:
>
> http://www.taylorswiftplanet.com/taylor-swift-biography.html
>
> Her personal website:
>
> https://www.taylorswift.com/
>
> Remember to make notes of new words you find while reading these webpages.

Section B, Unit 6, Lesson 1 - Adjectives - Antonyms

What are Antonyms?

In Unit 5 we met synonyms; words with the same or similar meaning. Now we move on to antonyms; words with opposite meanings. Antonyms can be nouns, verbs, adverbs or adjectives. In this unit we will focus on adjectives and learn them in pairs. Sometimes one word of a pair will be an adjective we have already learned. Notice that some of the new words are compounds and some use the adjective suffixes we have already met. The examples will continue the theme of personality.

Example

Extrovert   synonym: lively, **outgoing**   antonym: **introvert**

It is helpful to learn new words in groups like this.

Light-hearted (adj.) **lahyt-hahr**-tid
Serious-minded (adj.) **seer**-ee-*uh* s-**mahyn**-did
Describes somebody who is serious about a task or topic and rarely laughs or relaxes.
Example
Some religious people are serious minded because they believe that amusements are sinful.

Assertive (adj.) *uh*-**sur**-tiv
Describes somebody who is self-confident, puts forward their own point of view but also respects the rights of others.
Submissive (adj.) s*uh* b-**mis**-iv
Describes somebody who is obedient and does not argue.
Example
Some university and company interviewers prefer assertive candidates and reject submissive ones.

Diplomatic (adj.) dip-l*uh*-**mat**-ik
Describes somebody who is good at dealing with sensitive issues without causing offense.
Blunt (adj.) bluhnt
Describes somebody who says what they think directly and does not care about causing offense.
<u>Example</u>
It is sometimes claimed that women tend to be more diplomatic and less blunt than men.

Charismatic (adj) kar-iz-**mat**-ik
Colorless (adj) **kuhl**-er-les
(Describing personality) A person who is dull and does not have a strong personality.
<u>Example</u>
Celebrities are usually charismatic because colorless people do not attract attention.

Easy-going (adj.) **ee**-zee-**goh**-ing
Describes somebody who does not make big issues out of minor disagreements and is generally calm and easy to get on with.
Demanding (adj.) dih-**man**-ding, -**mahn**
Describes somebody who always expects more than others think is reasonable; someone who can be difficult to work with.
<u>Example</u>
Some experts think managers should be more demanding to raise productivity but others argue that a more easy-going style gets better results.

Passionate (adj.) **pash**-*uh*-nit
Describes somebody who shows strong feelings; somebody who is very enthusiastic about a subject or hobby.
Apathetic (ad.j) ap-*uh*-**thet**-ik
Describes somebody who does not have strong feelings; somebody who does not care about a subject or hobby.
<u>Example</u>
Some people are passionate about the computer game Fortnite and play every night but others are apathetic towards computer games and would rather hang out with friends.

Power up your Vocabulary

Section B, Unit 6, Lesson 2 - Antonyms with Prefixes - Critical Thinking

What are Prefixes?

In earlier units we have met suffixes; endings of words which tell you the part of speech and sometimes part of the meaning. Now we move on to prefixes; the beginnings of words. There are many types but the largest group are **negative prefixes.** These are commonly adjectives and often part of a pair of antonyms.

Prefixes introduced in this unit:

Dis ……   Il……..   Im………….   In…………   Ir……………   Un……………..

Organized (adj.) awr-g*uh*-nahyzd
Disorganized (adj.) dis-**awr**-g*uh*-nahyzd

Describing something that has/has not been arranged or planned.

Example
In writing tests examiners look for well organized answers whereas disorganized essays lose marks.

Logical (adj.) **loj**-i-k*uh* l
Illogical (adj.) ih-**loj**-i-k*uh* l

Describing something which does or does not follow the rules of logic in which claims are based on true ideas or facts.

Example
It is illogical to reach a conclusion which is contrary to the evidence.

Probable (adj.) **prob**-*uh*-b*uh* l
Improbable (adj.) im-**prob**-*uh*-b*uh* l

Describes something which is likely or unlikely to be true or to occur.

Example
It was improbable that Leicester City would win the English Premiership but they did.

Rational (adj.) **rash**-*uh*-nl
Irrational (adj.) ih-**rash**-*uh*-nl

Describes an idea or person that does or does not follow reason.

Example
The scientific revolution of the 17th and 18th centuries was based on rational thinking.

Proven (adj.) proo-ven
Unproven (adj.) *uh* n-proo-ven

Describes something which is or is not shown to be true by the evidence and rules of logic.

Example
In criminal law a defendant has to be proven guilty by the evidence before being sent to prison.

Power up your Vocabulary

Vocabulary in Use 1

The same word can have both a prefix and a suffix.

The suffixes ……able ……… ible mean can/have the ability to.
Combined with a negative prefix they mean can't/unable to.

A capable person can do something.
An **incapable** person cannot do something.

Vocabulary in Use 2

Spelling with negative prefixes and the suffixes …able and …ible can be tricky. Words beginning with L and R take the prefix ending with the same letter. But there are no other simple rules. Don't guess the prefix or suffix, use a dictionary.

Inevitable (adj.) in-**ev**-i-tuh-buh l
Describes something which must happen and cannot be avoided.
Example
Karl Marx claimed that it was inevitable that capitalism would be overthrown and replaced by communism.
(In critical thinking, claims that something is inevitable should be viewed with caution.)

Unacceptable (adj.) *uh* n ak-**sep**-t*uh*-b*uh* l
Describes something which cannot be regarded as OK or believed to have any **credibility**.
Example
Logical fallacies meant that the professor decided the student's **dissertation** was unacceptable.

Impenetrable (adj.) im-**pen**-i-tr*uh*-b*uh* l
(In critical thinking) Describes something which cannot be analyzed or understood.
Example
The student failed his **assignment** because his grammar was so poor that his argument was impenetrable.

Irreversible (adj.) ir-i-**vur**-s*uh*-b*uh* l
Describes something which can never be returned to its previous state.
Example
The greatest scientists and thinkers bring about irreversible changes in the way we see the world.

Illegible (adj.) ih-**lej**-*uh*-b*uh* l
Describes something, usually handwriting, which cannot be read.
Example
The writing in some ancient manuscripts is illegible.

Power up your Vocabulary

Section B, Unit 6, Exercises

Exercise 1: Antonym Bingo

Which 3 of the following 4 bingo cards have a correct line of 2 pairs of antonyms (opposites) from this unit? Lines may be horizontal, vertical or diagonal (see example).

(The first one has been done for you).

Example

a)

probable	serious minded	rational	irrational
illegible	improbable	introvert	passionate
assertive	light hearted	easy-going	blunt
extrovert	irreversible	apathetic	demanding

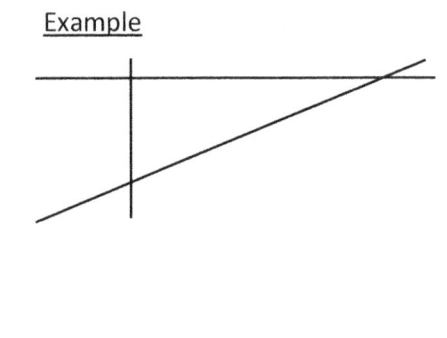

b)

light-hearted	colorless	passionate	rational
capable	incapable	organized	disorganized
legible	probable	irrational	diplomatic
introvert	submissive	legible	illegible

c)

serious-minded	rational	passionate	diplomatic
unacceptable	demanding	apathetic	disorganized
inevitable	assertive	irrational	blunt
proven	submissive	illegible	capable

d)

submissive	impenetrable	apathetic	improbable
unacceptable	demanding	passionate	acceptable
inevitable	easy-going	irrational	disorganized
unproven	assertive	rational	logical

Power up your Vocabulary

Exercise 2: Multiple Choice

Choose the best answer for each of the following questions:

Example

(d) Which of the following words is an antonym for charismatic:
    a) exciting   b) passionate   c) famous   d) colorless

1. (   ) Which of the following words describes something which is not based on reason:

    a) dislogical   b) unacceptable   c) irrational   d) unrational

2. (   ) Which of the following is not a negative prefix:

    a) uni   b) ir   c) dis   e) im

3. (   ) Which of the following is the best definition of a demanding manager:

    a) Someone who is relaxed about everything in the office.

    b) Someone who always expects more from his staff than they can deliver.

    c) Someone who is enthusiastic about his job and put his heart and soul into it.

    d) Who is always having fun and making jokes at work.

4. (   ) Which of the following words means something which is guaranteed to happen and cannot be stopped:

    a) irrational   b) illogical   c) inevitable   d) unevitable

5. (   ) Which of the following is not a characteristic of an assertive person:

    a) Someone who is not afraid to put forward their own point of view.

    b) Someone who respects others

    c) Someone who has self-belief

    d) Someone who always does as they are told.

6. (   ) Which two of the following combinations of prefix and suffix means can't/unable to:

  (   ) a) un ….. ment   b) ir ……. ible   c) dis ………… ic   d) in ….. able

Power up your Vocabulary

Exercise 3: Find the Mistake

Correct the misuses of vocabulary in the following sentences. Rewrite the sentence in the space provided so that it is grammatically correct and makes sense. The first one has been done for you.

1. Membership of the WTO is supposed to be illeversible.

Membership of the WTO is supposed to be <u>irreversible</u>.

2. Examiners prefer disorganized essays.

....

3. A serious minded person is one who laughs all the time.

....

4. It is unprobable that there is life on another planet in our **solar system**.

....

5. Diplomatic people frequently cause offense.

....

6. A criminal can only be convicted when the case against him/her is unproven.

....

7. Dismissive people obey orders without argument or discussion.

....

8. A prefix is the ending of a word.

....

Power up your Vocabulary

Section B, Unit 7, Lesson 1- Process Verbs and Collocations

> ### What are Collocations?
>
> Collocations are words often used together. There are several types, but in this unit, we will focus on collocations of verbs and nouns. These are widely used in business and industry to talk about the process of making or doing something.
>
> Some verbs have a dependent preposition between the verb and the noun. Make notes.
>
> Collocations differ from compounds in that the two words remain different parts of speech and are never joined or hyphenated.

Broadcast (v) (T) **brawd**-kast + radio or TV programs.
To send out programs on air to peoples' homes.
Example
The CNN broadcast the first TV pictures in 1922.

Demolish (v) (T) dih-**mol**-ish + a building
To knock down something.
Example
It is often necessary to demolish old buildings in order to redevelop cities.

Enrich (v) (T) en-**rich** + uranium
To improve the quality of something.
Example
Countries which can enrich uranium can produce nuclear weapons.

Excavate (v) (T) **eks**-k*uh*-veyt + a site
To dig carefully to find the remains of old buildings or people.
Example
The archaeologist Sir Mortimer Wheeler excavated the site of the tomb of King Tutankhamen.

Generate (v) (T) **jen**-*uh*-reyt + electricity
To produce or create profusely by a vital, natural process.
Example
Renewable energy such as solar, wind or wave power is increasingly being used to generate electricity.

Power up your Vocabulary

Harvest (v) (T) **hahr**-vist + crops
(In agriculture) To cut and gather plants or catch fish or animals for food.
Example
Genetically Modified foods sometimes allow farmers to harvest two or three crops per year.

Incinerate (v) (T) in-**sin**-*uh*-reyt + waste
To destroy something by burning it.
Example
A lot of medical waste has to be incinerated to prevent the spread of infectious diseases.

Mine (v) (T) mahyn + coal/copper
(In industry) To dig a deep hole in the ground in order to extract minerals.
Example
Mining coal provided the main source of energy for the first industrial revolution.

Vocabulary in Use

Some English verbs have a dependent preposition between the verb and the noun. You will improve your English more quickly if you make notes of these when you are learning new words.

Drill for (v) (T) dril + oil
To make a hole in the ground using a revolving tool with sharp edges and a pointed end.
Example
As the world begins to run out of oil, companies will have to drill for new sources in the deep ocean or Antarctica.

Engage with (v) (T) en-**geyj** + customers, employees
To talk to and listen to people on an equal basis in order to occupy their attention.
Example
Human resources professionals are realizing that companies have to engage with their staff to improve morale and **motivation**.

Filter out (v) (T) **fil**-ter + impurities
To pour a liquid through a tool with very small holes called a sieve in order to remove large particles.
Example
Water treatment processes filter out impurities in order to make the water fit to drink.

Power up your Vocabulary

Section B, Unit 7, Lesson 2 - New Collocations - Digital Business

> ### Vocabulary in Use
>
> In Unit 3 we saw how compounds are used to make new words to keep the English language up to date with developments in technology and society. New collocations are formed in the same way. In this lesson we will look at some examples of verbs we have already met and some new ones used in new collocations.

Mine (v) (T) mahyn + data
To analyze data deeply to find hidden patterns in the information.
Example
Recently a lot of companies have begun to mine big data in order to gain insights into their customers' preferences and consumer behavior.

Enhance (v) (T) en-**hans** + experience, understanding
To improve the quality of something or add value to it.
Example
Many retailers are trying to enhance customer experience to encourage more shoppers to visit their stores instead of shopping online.

Generate (v) (T) **jen**-*uh*-reyt + ideas, insights
To actively create and distribute something.
Example
Many organizations are turning to think tanks and focus groups to generate new ideas and insights.

Filter (v) (T) **fil**-ter + content
To check content and remove items judged to be offensive or illegal.
Example
Social Media Platforms such as Facebook are under increasing pressure from governments and lobby groups to filter content uploaded to their platforms.

Power up your Vocabulary

> **Study Tip**
>
> The collocations in this unit are not a complete list.
> It is a good idea to make notes of additional collocations you find in reading using spider grams.
>
> transmit — data
> transmit — diseases
> transmit — electronic signals
>
> Always try to write example sentences of your own e.g.
>
> Fiber optic broadband cables can transmit gigabytes of data in microseconds.

Advocate (v) (T) **ad**-v*uh*-keyt + policy
To argue for or recommend something in public.
Example
More and more people advocate sustainable development policies for businesses and society.

Power up (v) (T) **pou**-er - uhp + a project
To allocate extra resources (money, people etc) to something in order to complete if faster.
Example
The British government has just decided to power up construction of a new runway at Heathrow.

Livestream (v) (T) **liv**-streem + an event, sport
To broadcast something on the internet as it happens.
Example
It is becoming essential to livestream sporting events to attract younger viewers.

Digitize (v) (T) **dij**-i-tahyz + documents, manuscripts, records
To convert traditional media into a form which can be uploaded to the internet and read on electronic devices.
Example
Family history societies have digitized millions of old records to make them accessible from anywhere in the world via the internet.

Section B, Unit 7, Exercises

Exercise 1: Multiple Choice

Choose the best answer for each of the following questions. The first one has been done for you.

1. (*b*) Which of the following nouns does not collocate with *transmit*:
   a) diseases   b) *projects*   c) data   d) electronic signals

2. (   ) Which of the following nouns does collocate with the verb *mine*:
   a) steel   b) oil   c) electricity   d) coal

3. (   ) Which preposition is required between the verb *drill* and its object:
   a) to   b) for   c) at   d) from

4. (   ) What is often demolished:
   a) a building   b) a TV program   c) a farmer's crop   d) a coal mine

5. (   ) Which two of the following nouns can collocate with the verb *filter*:
   (   ) a) digital content   b) electricity   c) energy   d) liquids

6. (   ) In which academic subject is the verb *excavate* often used:
   a) economics   b) computer science   c) maths   d) archaeology

7. (   ) The noun *policy* is often preceded by which verb:
   a) advocate   b) advise   c) accuse   d) assert

8. (   ) To enrich something e.g. uranium means:
   a) make it weaker   b) ban it   c) make it stronger or purer   d) look for it

Exercise 2: Cloze Test

Complete the collocations in the following passage from a business blog. Use words from this unit found in the word bank. Number 1 has been done to help you.

Word Bank

broadcast   advocate   ideas/insights
engage   mine   transmit   experience

Power up your Vocabulary

Modern business is changing faster than ever before. No longer is it simply about making a product and selling it for as much profit as possible. Stakeholders, particularly customers and employees, are becoming ever more demanding and difficult to attract and retain. Companies have to (1) *engage* with their staff to keep them motivated. Customers expect to be treated as special individuals. When modern customers visit a shopping center or e commerce website they want to do more than just buy products. Businesses need to offer something to enhance consumers (2) .... To achieve this businesses have to collect and (3) .... huge amounts of data to learn about customers individual preferences. Usually the data is stored and processed in the cloud which means they need to (4) .... it via high speed broadband. Customers are also increasingly concerned about the ethics and sustainability of businesses. More and more business leaders (5) .... environmentally friendly policies because customers may refuse to buy from businesses which do not respect the environment. Changing the traditional way in which businesses think and operate requires innovation. More and more companies are looking to think tanks or focus groups to generate new (6) .... and using the internet to reach customers instead of making advertisements to (7) .... on TV or radio. A lot of businesses are struggling to adapt to all these changes and there is little doubt that the business revolution has only just begun.

Exercise 3: Verb Replacement

Replace the underlined everyday verbs in the following sentences with a more specific process verb from this unit. The first one has been done for you.

1. *Advocate* A lot of people <u>suggest</u> sustainable development policies.

2. .... Countries today try to <u>get</u> as much electricity as possible from renewable sources.

3. .... Some countries have been accused of trying to <u>improve</u> their stores of uranium in order to make nuclear weapons.

4. .... Genetically modified foods mean that some farmers can <u>collect</u> more crops to help feed the rising global population.

5. .... Companies such as BP and Exxon Mobil <u>make</u> holes in the seabed to look for more oil.

6. .... Conservationists have objected to plans to <u>pull down</u> old parts of the city.

7. .... Plans to <u>put</u> more World War One soldier's diaries online have been welcomed by historians.

Power up your Vocabulary

Section B, Unit 8, Lesson 1 - Reporting Verbs - Social Sciences

What are Reporting Verbs?

Reporting verbs are used to introduce what somebody else has said or done. We use them in everyday speech e.g. David said that ……. , Susan replied that ………. A much wider range of reporting verbs are used in academic writing and news reporting. Note that all reporting verbs are transitive (must have an object). Many of them have subtle connotations of meaning. Younger and less educated readers often miss these.

In this unit we will look at some reporting verbs in the context of examples from the social sciences. On this page we will look at words with positive connotations.

Announce (v) (T) *uh-***nouns**
To tell large numbers of people something officially.
Example
The government have announced increased spending on social housing in today's budget.

Assert (v) (T) *uh-***surt**
To put forward a claim or point of view, usually strongly.
Example
Neoliberal economists assert that any interference with the free market is wrong.

Attribute (v) (T) *uh-***trib**-yoot
To give credit or blame for something to others.
Example
Giving evidence to the public inquiry Professor Smith attributed blame for the recent riots to the police.

Disclose (v) (T) dih-**sklohz**
To make public something which was previously secret.
Example
Recently opened archives have disclosed new information about past preparations for nuclear war.

Hypothesize (v) (T) hahy-**poth**-*uh*-sahyz
To suggest a theory which might explain something, usually intended to be the subject of further research and discussion.
Example
Some scientists hypothesize that climate change will cause some animal populations to migrate to new habitats.

Correlate (v) (T)
To calculate the relationship between two or more things.
Example
In the social sciences researchers correlate large amounts of data to look for patterns of cause and effect.

> ## Vocabulary in Use
>
> Reporting verbs are nearly always transitive (they require an object). The structure may be:
>
> a) Subject + reporting verb + *that* + *a statement of what is being reported.*
> b) Statement of what is being reported + reporting verb + subject.
>
> Examples
> Professor Patel stated that there has been a welcome fall in teenage sugar consumption.
> Teenage sugar consumption has shown a welcome fall, stated Professor Patel.
>
> On this page we will look at a group of reporting verbs which indicate that the writer or speaker is going to disagree with what is being reported.

Deny (v) (T) dih-**nahy**
To state that something is not true, often used about allegations of wrongdoing.
Example
The presidential candidate denied allegations of corruption reported in yesterday's newspapers.

Dispute (v) (T) dih-**spyoot**
To disagree about something.
Example
Historians continue to dispute the causes of the First World War.

Reject (v) (T) ri-**jekt**
To refuse to accept something. Often used about proposals or recommendations.
Example
The Directors rejected the proposed merger with ARD Corporation.

Retort (v) (I) ri-**tawrt**
Used in conversation or debate. To reply quickly and in anger, sometimes with humor or sarcasm.
Example
"Don't be ridiculous" the Secretary of State retorted during angry exchanges in Parliament today.

Power up your Vocabulary

Section B, Unit 8, Lesson 2 - Verbs in Critical Thinking

> ## Vocabulary in Use
>
> Verbs are often used in critical thinking to report the function of arguments, experiments or evidence. Knowing the meaning of these verbs will improve your ability to actively engage with and question what you read. They will also help you write in a more mature, academic style.

Assume (v) (T) *uh*-**soom**
To believe something is true without thinking about it or having the evidence to prove it.
Example
In critical thinking it is important to understand what you are assuming to be true.

Imply (v) (T) im-**plahy**
To suggest that something is true without stating it directly.
Example
In some cultures, it is common for authors to imply a conclusion rather than state it openly especially on controversial topics.

Infer (v) (T) in-**fur**
To draw conclusions from evidence implied but not stated by an author.
Example
The ability to infer logically is an important critical reading skill often tested in examinations.

Justify (v) (T) **juhs**-t*uh*-fahy
To provide evidence to prove that an opinion, theory or hypothesis is true.
Example
Examiners usually require students to justify their opinions.

Refute (v) (T) ri-**fyoot**
To show why something is wrong. Often used of an opinion in critical thinking.
Example
The Economics lecturer refuted the arguments put forward by Anderson in his recent book on inflation.

Power up your Vocabulary

Word Families

In Unit 1 we learned the importance of acquiring new vocabulary in word families. This applies to reporting verbs as well. Nearly all reporting verbs have noun forms; often nominalisers. Some have other parts of speech as well. On this page we will look at some additional reporting verbs and extend them into word families. Learning these word families will help you use vocabulary flexibly in different grammatical structures.

Accuse (v) (T) *uh*-**kyooz** To say that somebody has done something morally or legally wrong.
Accusation (n) (u) ak-y*oo*-**zey**-sh*uh*n (statement).   **Accuser** (n) (c) *uh*-**kyoo**-zer (person)
Accusing (adj.) *uh*-**kyooz**-ing   **Accusingly** (adv) *uh*-**kyooz**-ingli

Example
The professor denied the accusation that he had falsified his results and threatened to sue his accuser.

Plagiarize (v) (T) **pley**-j*uh*-rahyz To use somebody else's words or ideas as if they were your own.
Plagiarism (n) (u) **pley**-j*uh*-riz-*uh*m (concept/practice)   **Plagiarizer** (n) (c) **pley**-j*uh*-rahyzer (person)
Plagiarized (adj.) **pley**-j*uh*-rahyzd

Examples
Fourteen students were expelled from the college yesterday after being found guilty of plagiarism. In some cases, essays they submitted were found to be up to 90% plagiarized.

Cite (v) (I) sahyt To give details in an academic text of the source of ideas or information used.
Citation (n) (c) sahy-**tey**-sh*uh*n (In writing) A reference to a particular source.

Examples
All western universities require students to cite sources in their writing using a variety of citation styles. Failure to do so may be regarded as plagiarism.

Verify (v) (T) **ver**-*uh*-fahy To prove that facts or information are true.
Verification (n) (process) ver-*uh*-fi-**key**-sh*uh*n
verifiable/unverifiable (adjs.)   **ver**-*uh*-fahy -**ey**-b*uh*l   un-**ver**-*uh*-fahy -**ey**-b*uh*l
verifiably (adv.)   **ver**-*uh*-fahy **ey**-blee

Examples
In scientific research, papers are often subject to a process of verification called peer review and published results should be verifiable by independent researchers.

Power up your Vocabulary

Section B, Unit 8, Exercises

Exercise 1: Words in the Nest

Birds raise their families in trees. How many words do you know to complete the families in these trees. Some words are in this unit but you will need to use a dictionary to find others. The first one has been done for you.

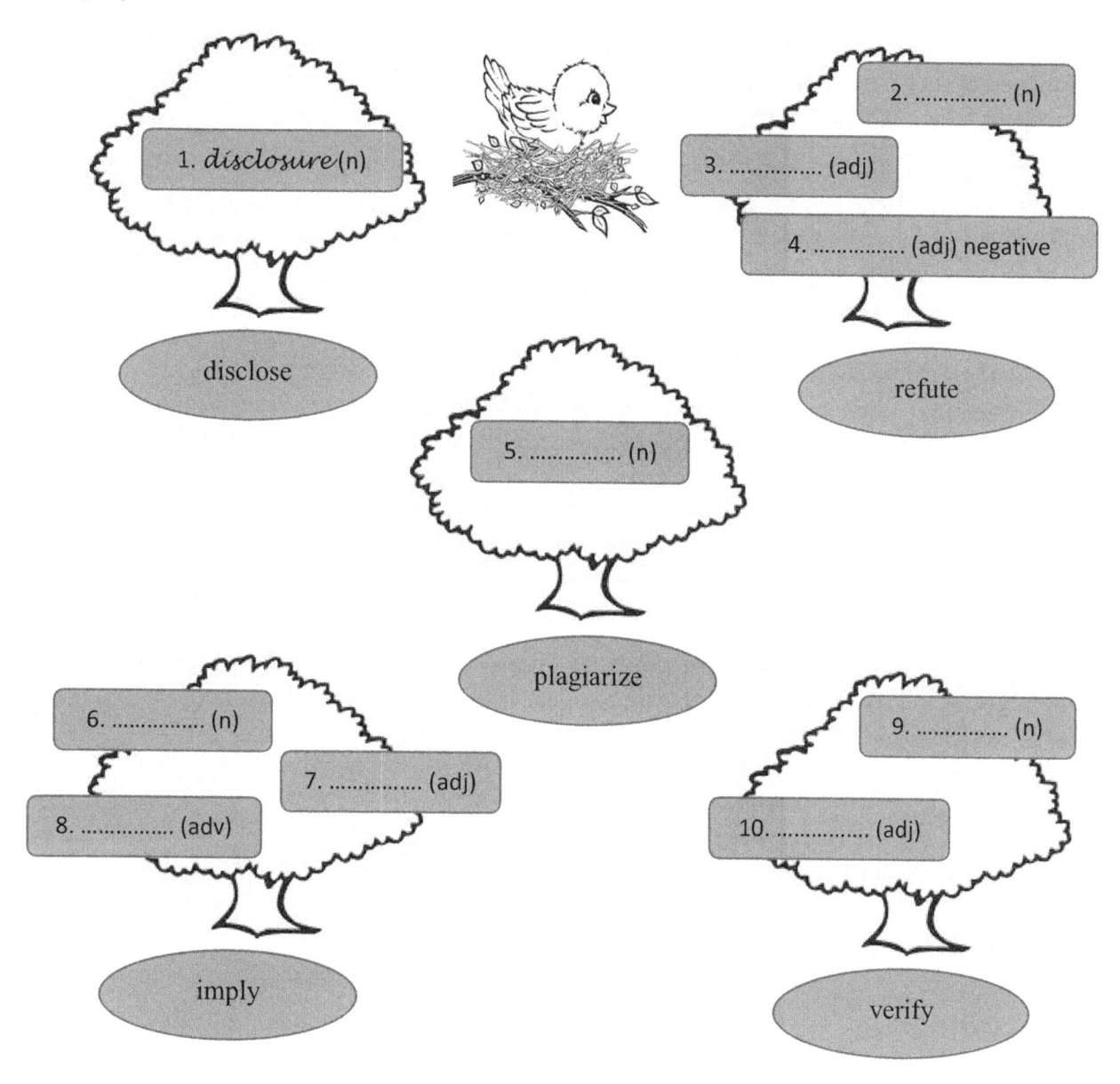

1. *disclosure* (n) — disclose

2. .... (n)
3. .... (adj)
4. .... (adj) negative
— refute

5. .... (n) — plagiarize

6. .... (n)
7. .... (adj)
8. .... (adv)
— imply

9. .... (n)
10. .... (adj)
— verify

Power up your Vocabulary

Exercise 2: Cloze Test

Fill in the blanks in the following passage from a high school study skills course manual. Use words from this unit. There are context clues to help you but be careful with parts of speech from word families. The first one has been done for you and the first letter of each word is provided to help you.

During their first year in senior high school students will be expected to become familiar with the basic techniques of critical thinking, develop active reading skills and become familiar with the basic procedures for academic research.

We will start with critical thinking. In critical thinking one of the first things to learn is how to recognize what we **(1)** *assume* to be true. We will then learn to **(2) j**.................. our assumptions and opinions. Next, we will look at evidence and consider how researchers can verify their **(3) h**.................. by using data. Sometimes this will involve using IT skills to analyze large amounts of data to look for patterns of cause and effect. Students will be required to master statistical techniques to measure the **(4) c**.................. involved. We will then look at conclusions. Students will learn to recognize not only the obvious conclusions but those which have to be **(5) i**.................. by the reader from evidence provided by an author. We will look at some conclusions from social science research which have been **(6) a**.................. recently and discuss what they **(7) i**.................. for future public policy.

Active reading involves engaging with a passage and applying critical thinking to evaluate the arguments put forward. We will study passages in which an author uses persuasive writing techniques to **(8) a** .... a strong position. But we will then go on to consider how another author can show that the opinion is wrong; in other words **(9) r**............. it by using critical thinking techniques.

In the last part of the course we will teach students internet-based research techniques, not only finding sources but the correct way to **(10) a**.................. them by using **(11) c**.................. in your essays and reports.

Power up your Vocabulary

Exercise 3: Crossword

Use words from this unit to do the crossword.

Across
4. Prove that something is true.
6. A claim that somebody has done something wrong.
7. Draw conclusions that are not explicitly stated by the author.
8. Make a claim strongly.

5. Disagree about something.

Down
1. State that an accusation is wrong.
3. Make public something that was formerly secret.

2. Refuse to agree to something.
6. Tell the public about something new.

Power up your Vocabulary

Section B, Unit 9, Lesson 1 - Phrasal Verbs

> ### What are Phrasal Verbs?
>
> Phrasal verbs are verbs which can be combined with prepositions or particles to make verbs with new meanings. They are generally idiomatic and more often used in speech than in writing, although that is changing especially in business English. A lot of phrasal verbs also have single word synonyms.
>
> There are several approaches to learning phrasal verbs. In this unit we will group them according to the main verb starting with expressions using **bring, do** and **make.**

Bring down (v) (T) (inclusive)
To cause something to collapse or fail.
Example
The minister told his colleagues that going ahead with the new tax proposals would bring down the government.

Bring round (v) (T) (inclusive)
To change somebody's mind about an issue.
Example
After an excellent presentation Karen brought the class round to her point of view.

Do away with (v) (T) (exclusive)   synonym: abolish
To end something.
Example
The meeting decided to do away with traditional shops entirely and sell everything online.

Do out of (v) (T) (inclusive)   synonym: cheat
To deny something to a person that they have a right to.
Example
The trade unions believe the company is trying to do the workers out of their pension rights as part of the merger deal.

Make up for (v) (T) (exclusive)   synonym: compensate
To do something to compensate for a loss somebody has suffered which was your fault.
Example
The lawyers say we will have to do something to make up for our customers losing access to their bank accounts for two days after the computer systems crashed.

Power up your Vocabulary

Vocabulary in Use

Phrasal verbs nearly always have an object. But there are two main types of phrasal verbs depending on where the object goes in the sentence.

Inclusive phrasal verbs
With inclusive phrasal verbs the object can come between the **verb** and the **preposition or particle.**
e.g. The company is trying to **do** the workers **out of** ……….

When the object is a pronoun it must always come between the verb and the preposition/particle.

Exclusive phrasal verbs
Exclusive phrasal verbs always have the object after the **preposition or particle**.
e.g. The CFO stated that the police are going to look **into** the accusations of fraud.

Go off (v) (T)
To lose interest in something.
Example: Reports say that Davis Ltd have gone off the idea of entering the Chinese market due to the ongoing trade war.

Go through with (v) (T)   synonyms: complete, finish
To finish something despite opposition.
Example: The board decided to go through with the plans to close the Newcastle factory despite the threat of a strike.

Look up (v) (T)   synonym: improve
To improve.
Example: The marketing director told the meeting that sales are looking up.

Look back on (v) (T)
To reflect and learn lessons from something which happened in the past.
Example: A lot of older people in Britain look back on the past with nostalgia and wish today's schools were run the way they used to be.

Section B, Unit 9, Lesson 2 - Phrasal Verbs in Context

> ## Vocabulary in Use
>
> Some books refer to phrasal verbs as "two-word verbs". This is misleading. Some phrasal verbs have both a preposition and a particle, so have three words e.g. look back on. Most phrasal verbs can also be used in a range of tenses. Auxiliary verbs may also make the structure more than two words e.g. Davis Ltd have gone off …. (present perfect tense).
>
> We will see more examples as we look at phrasal verbs formed with **get, pull** and **put.**

Get behind (v) (T) (exclusive)
To unite in agreement with something and support it in public.
Example
The principal urged all the teachers and pupils to get behind the new school code of discipline and raise standards.

Get down to (v) (T) (exclusive)
Become serious and focused about something.
Example
The chairperson said "Look, we have already wasted half an hour, let's get down to business."

Get out of (v) (T) (inclusive)
To avoid a responsibility or legal obligation.
Example
The football club are considering how to get out of their contract with their star striker after his latest love affair caused another scandal.

Pull out (v) (T) (inclusive)   synonyms: leave, quit
To leave something.
Example
XYZ Corporation has pulled out of the planned merger with Autovision Inc.

Put forward (v) (T) (inclusive)
To suggest, propose, recommend or **advocate** something.
Example
The Vice President of marketing put forward a plan to **enhance** the company's presence on social media.

Study Tip: Phrasal Verbs in Context

Many phrasal verbs can have completely different meanings depending on the context.

Examples

Go off (an idea) = lose interest in it.   Go off (food) = become rotten and unfit to eat.

When you are learning new phrasal verbs, it is vital to make notes of a complete example sentence or context, not just the word in isolation.

On this page we will look at some more examples of multiple meanings using other verbs we have not considered so far.

Break down (v) (T) (inclusive)
1. To stop working e.g. a car, a machine.
2. To divide something into its component parts e.g. a complex project.

Example

Project management software can be very useful for breaking down a complex task into achievable sections.

Knock down (v) (T) (inclusive)
1. To strike to the ground.
2. To reduce the price of something.

Example

The company is on the edge of bankruptcy, so we have to knock down our prices.

See through (v) (T) (exclusive)
1. To look through something transparent e.g. glass.
2. To not be deceived by something or somebody.

Example

Consumers quickly saw through the false claims the company made about its environmental standards.

Fill in (v) (T) (inclusive)
1. To put earth back into a hole.
2. To complete an **application** form.
3. To substitute for somebody e.g. a sick colleague.

Example

The head teacher asked the staff meeting for a volunteer to fill in for Mrs Jackson who was sick.

Section B, Unit 9, Exercises

Exercise 1: Memory Game

Play this game with a classmate or study partner. You will need a pair of dice. The first player throws both dice. Look at the instruction below for the number you throw. Write down the phrasal verbs shown. You have 30 seconds per turn. Don't look back to the text. Continue until all the instructions have been used up. The player with the most correct words wins. The first one has been done for you.

Number on the dice	Instructions	Answers
2	Write down four phrasal verbs with the preposition **down**	*Knock down*
		....
		....
		....
3	Write down one phrasal verb with the preposition **away**	....
4	Write down four phrasal verbs with the preposition **out**	....
		....
		....
		....
5	Write down two phrasal verbs with the preposition **up**	....
		....
6	Write down one phrasal verb with the preposition **off**	....
7	Write down two phrasal verbs with the preposition **through**	....
		....
8	Write down one phrasal verb with the preposition **back**	....
9	Write down one phrasal verb with the preposition **behind**	....
10	Write down one phrasal verb with the preposition **forward**	....
11	Write down one phrasal verb with the preposition **round**	....
12	Write down one phrasal verb with the preposition **in**	....

Power up your Vocabulary

Exercise 2: Matching Sentence Halves

Match the halves to make complete sentences. The first one has been done for you.

Your answers   a + h   b + ……..   c + ……….   d + ……….   e + ……..

a) After a powerful campaign the Peoples' Party brought *round*

f) all the overtime you have done this weekend.

b) We'll give you two days off next week to make up for

g) settling my parents claim for flood damage.

c) The team has worked much better since the leader broke down

h) public opinion to support reducing the voting age to 16.

d) Our insurance company is trying to get out of

i) instead of Spanish was a mistake.

e) When I look back on it, studying economics

j) our term project into manageable stages.

Exercise 3: Meanings in Context

Choose the correct meaning for the underlined phrasal verb in each sentence. The first one has been done for you.

1. (*b*) The librarian has gone to <u>look up</u> the date when the book I need for my essay is due back.

    a) The librarian raised her head to look the speaker in the eye.
    b) The librarian went to check some information.
    c) The librarian wanted to improve my essay.

2. (   ) The restaurant has lost a lot of money because a power cut to the refrigerators meant that a lot of food <u>went off</u>.

    a) The restaurant owners changed their minds.
    b) The food became unfit for human consumption.

3. (   ) Greenwashing means claiming that something is environmentally friendly when it is not but consumers soon <u>see through</u> such advertising.

    a) Consumers do not believe advertisements containing greenwashing.
    b) Consumers look though a virtual reality screen to see the advertisements.

4. (   ) The headteacher announced that every student who wishes to go on this summer's field trip to Italy must <u>fill in</u> and return their application form by tomorrow morning.

    a) Students must complete a form.
    b) Students must substitute for sick classmates if they wish to go on the school trip.

5. (   ) My sister missed an important meeting yesterday because she <u>knocked down</u> a boy on the way. He was not seriously injured but she was too upset to continue.

    a) The speaker's sister was scared to attend the meeting in case she was asked to repeat her proposal again.
    b) The speaker's sister had an accident in her car.

Power up your Vocabulary

Section B, Unit 10, Lesson 1 - Describing Trends

Trend (n + v) trend
A long-term change in direction, to change direction over the long term.
<u>Example</u>
Average life expectancy has been on an upward trend for many years.

> ## Vocabulary in Use
>
> In middle schools and high schools most subjects become more quantitative. Students learn to collect data, draw graphs and charts themselves and analyze graphs and charts found in textbooks. To do this you need to learn vocabulary used to describe and present data.
>
> There are two main structures: a) verb + adverb   b) article + adjective + noun
>
> In this unit we will learn verbs and adverbs. But remember most of the new words in this unit come in word families and also have noun and adjective forms

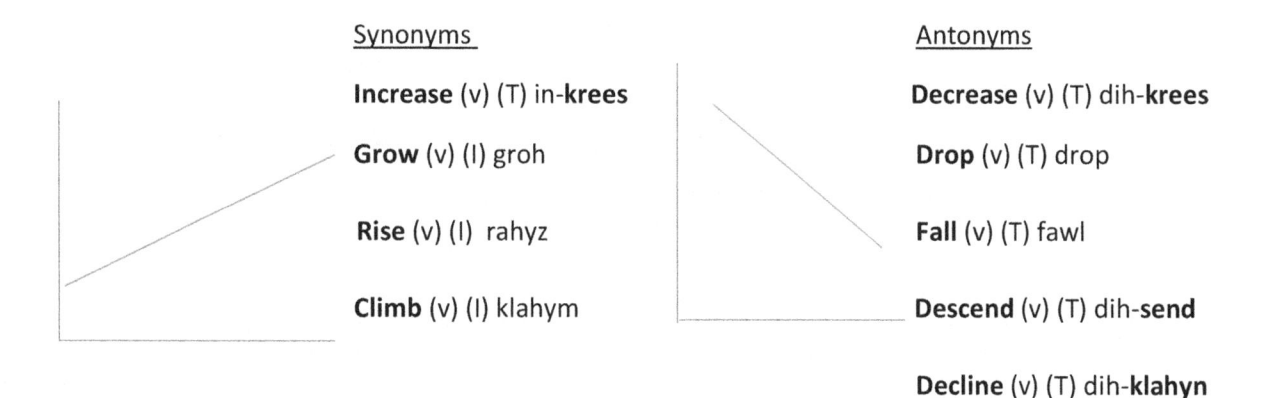

<u>Synonyms</u>

Increase (v) (T) in-**krees**

Grow (v) (I) groh

Rise (v) (I) rahyz

Climb (v) (I) klahym

<u>Antonyms</u>

Decrease (v) (T) dih-**krees**

Drop (v) (T) drop

Fall (v) (T) fawl

Descend (v) (T) dih-**send**

Decline (v) (T) dih-**klahyn**

Study Tip

You may know some of these words but having many synonyms available is important for fluent writing of this nature, so concentrate on learning words you have not used before.

<u>Examples</u>

In some countries such as Japan the percentage of the population aged over 65 is increasing/growing/rising/ascending very quickly.

The fertility rate (the number of babies born per 1000 women) is decreasing/dropping/falling/declining in most parts of the world.

Power up your Vocabulary

Vocabulary in Use

Trends do not always simply go up or down. There is sometimes no clear pattern. In other situations, trends can change direction. On this page we will look at some verbs for describing data in these scenarios. Notice that some of them are phrasal verbs similar to those we learned in Unit 9.

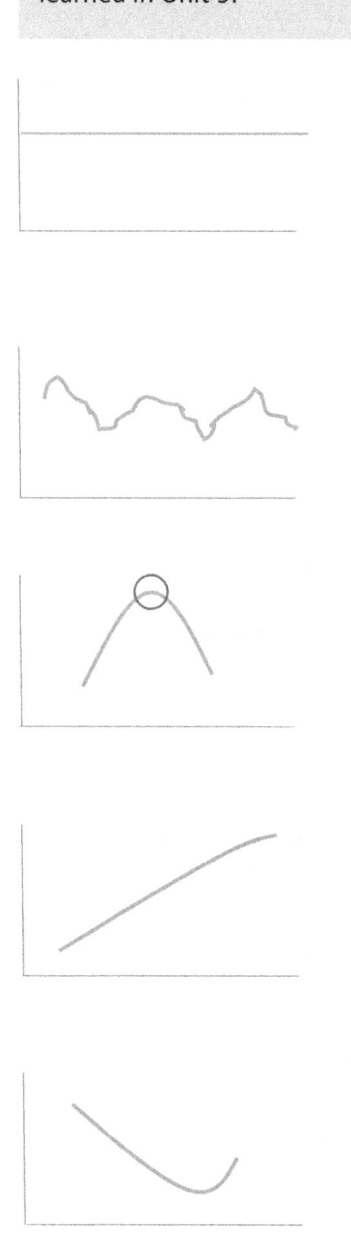

Stay constant (v + n)
To remain the same over a period of time.
Example
The temperatures during a heatwave may stay constant for a week or more.

Fluctuate (v) (I) **fluhk**-choo-eyt
To vary without any clear pattern or direction.
Example
Temperatures in the UK fluctuate from day to day.

Peak (v) (I) peek
To reach the maximum value during a period of time.
Example
In India average monthly rainfall peaks during the monsoon season.

Level off (v) (I) **lev**-*uh* l-**awf**
To stop increasing or decreasing or do so more slowly.
Example
Experts say that the rate of global warming has to level off by the middle of the 21st century if disaster is to be averted.

Rebound (v) (I) ri-**bound**
To begin increasing again after a period of decline.
Example
The population of wild pandas has rebounded in recent years thanks to conservation efforts.

Power up your Vocabulary

Section B, Unit 10, Lesson 2 - Adding Adverbs

Why Use Adverbs?

Adverbs are words which modify a verb or an adjective, not a noun. In this unit we will look at adverbs which modify a verb. They tell you something about the way in which the action of the verb happens. When we are talking about trends adverbs tell us something about how change occurs. This may be:

The extent of change.   The speed of change.   The sequence of change.

We will learn examples of each in this lesson. Understanding them will improve your vocabulary as well as your reading and writing.

The Extent of Change

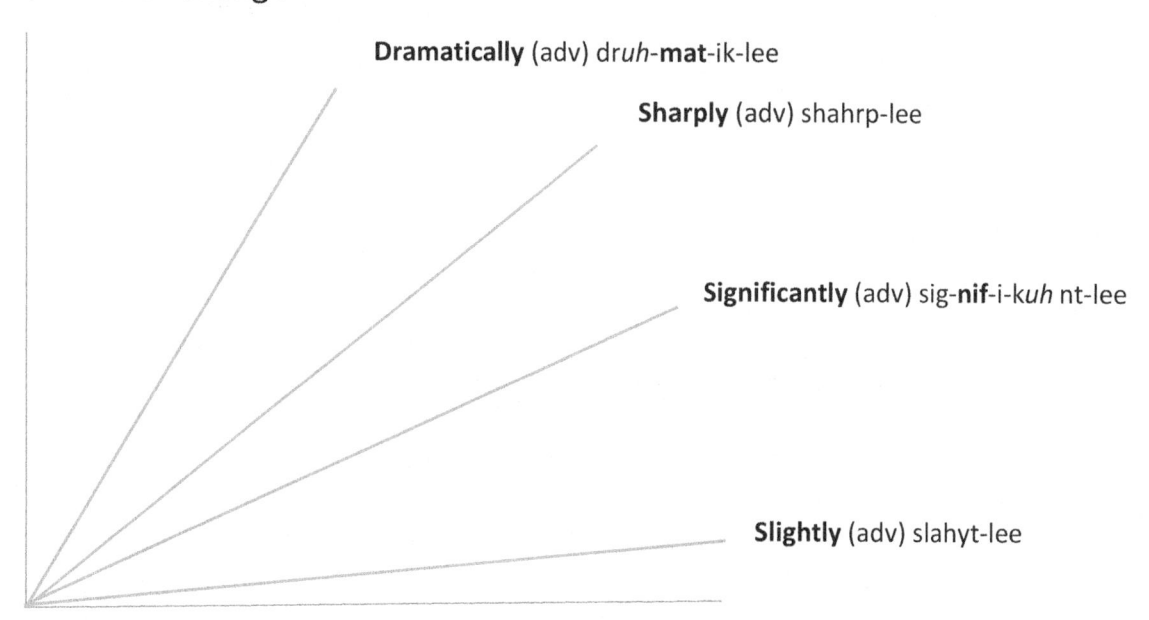

Dramatically (adv) dr*uh*-**mat**-ik-lee

Sharply (adv) shahrp-lee

Significantly (adv) sig-**nif**-i-k*uh* nt-lee

Slightly (adv) slahyt-lee

These adverbs can be combined with all the synonyms for increase and decrease in Lesson 1.

Examples

The number of extreme weather events such as heatwaves, droughts and hurricanes recorded has increased sharply in recent years, probably due to climate change.

The population of some American cities, such as Detroit, has fallen considerably in recent years due to changes in the local economy.

Power up your Vocabulary

The Speed of Change

Gradually (adv) **graj**-oo-*uh* lee
Happening over an extended period of time.
Example
In temperate climates the seasons change gradually.

Rapidly (adv) **rap**-id-lee
Happening quickly, over a short period of time.
Example
When barometric pressure falls rapidly weather forecasters know a storm is coming.

Constantly (adv) **kon**-st*uh* nt-lee
Change happening at the same speed over a period of time.
Example
The percentage of the world's population living in cities has been rising constantly for the last 50 years.

Vocabulary in Use

All these adverbs can be further refined by adding modifiers such as:

quite
very
extremely

Example
The population of Japan is expected to decline quite rapidly over the next few decades.

The Sequence of Change

Previously (adv) **pree**-vee-*uh* s-lee
An action or event which happened before another action or event.
Example
Before the Wenchuan earthquake in China in 2008 the area had previously been destroyed several times.

Simultaneously (adv) sahy-m*uh* l-**tey**-nee-*uh* s-lee
Two or more events or actions which occur at the same time. There may or may not be a cause and effect relationship between them.
Example
In some countries the birth rate is falling and simultaneously older people are living longer.

Subsequently (adv) **suhb**-si-kw*uh* nt-lee
An event or action which occurs after another event or action.
Example
The Montreal Protocol was signed in 1987. Subsequently CFC emissions fell sharply and the hole in the ozone layer began to repair itself.

Section B, Unit 10, Exercises

Exercise 1: Labelling Graphs and Charts

The following six graphs and tables show sales of six new technology products during their first year on the market. Write a short sentence to describe the main trend or trends. Use verbs and adverbs as appropriate in the past tense. The first one has been done for you.

1)

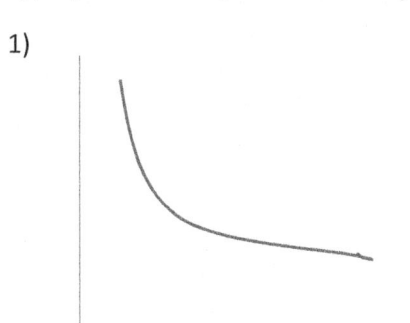

Sales fell dramatically before gradually levelling off

2)

....

3)

....

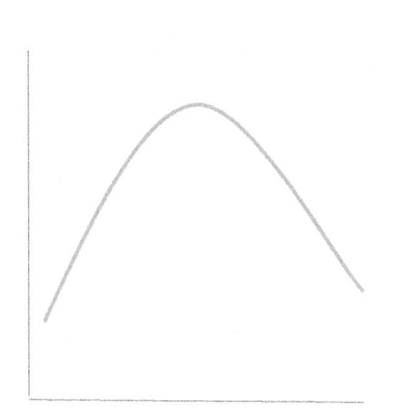

4)

....

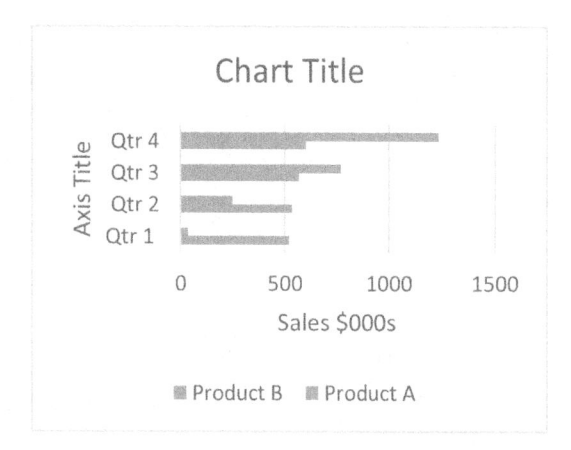

5)

....

6)

....

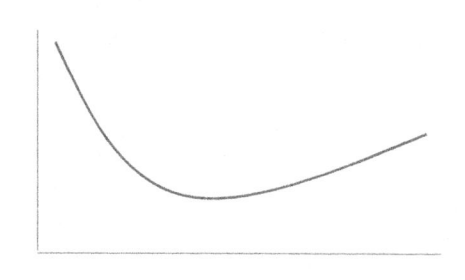

Exercise 2: Cloze Test

The graph below shows average monthly temperature and precipitation (rainfall) in the Indian city of Kolkota. Fill in the blanks in the description below using verbs and adverbs from this unit. The first one has been done for you and the first letter of each word is given to help you.

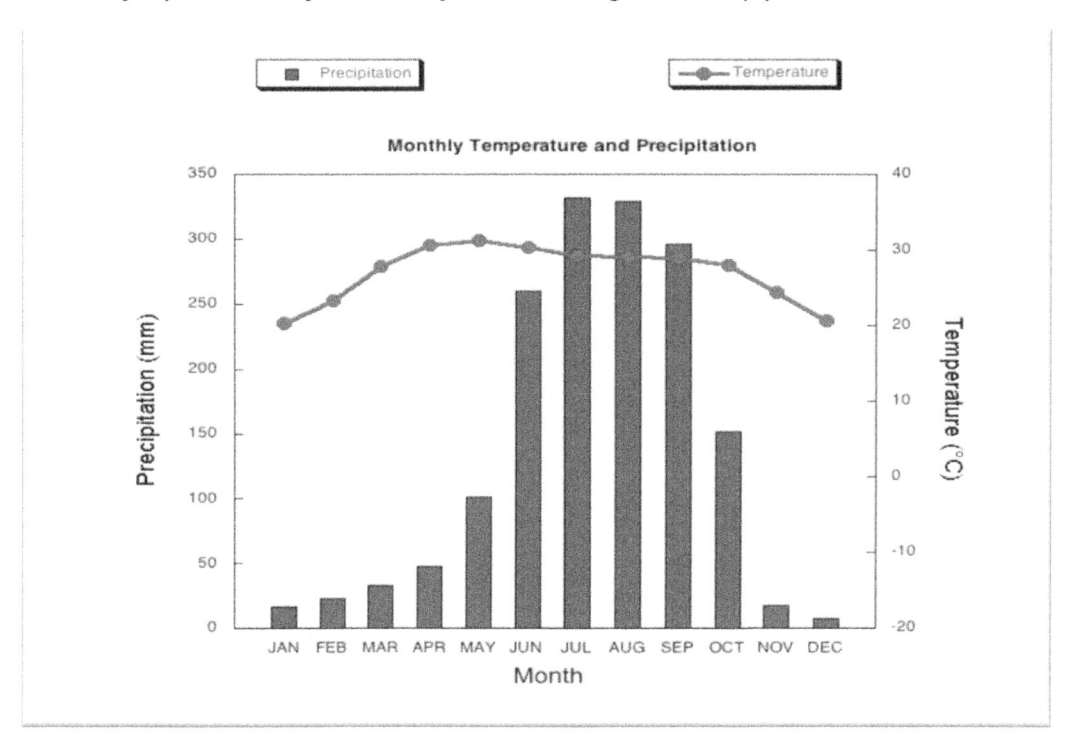

The graph illustrates the monthly average temperatures and the average amount of rainfall in Kolkota, India. It is clear that the climate is very hot throughout the year but rainfall is concentrated in the summer months.

To be more specific average temperatures rise (1) *significantly* in the spring from about 20 degrees C in January to a maximum of just over 30 in May. The weather then gets a little cooler in May and June. Temperatures stay more or less (2) **c** ………………… in the summer (July to September). (3) **S** ………………. there is a quite a significant fall from October to December.

India has a monsoon climate so rainfall is very low from January to April but then (4) **c**………… (5) **d** …………………………. in May and June before it (6) **p** ……………… at around 330 mm in July before an equally steep (7) **f**………. in September and October. In the winter months Kolkota receives less than 10 mm of rain per month.

Power up your Vocabulary

Exercise 3: Oral Presentation

Give a one-minute presentation in which you describe the graph below. You can either give your presentation to a partner face to face or record yourself using a cell phone. If you have a tutor ask him/her for feedback.

Overseas visitors to three different areas in a European country between 1987 and 2007

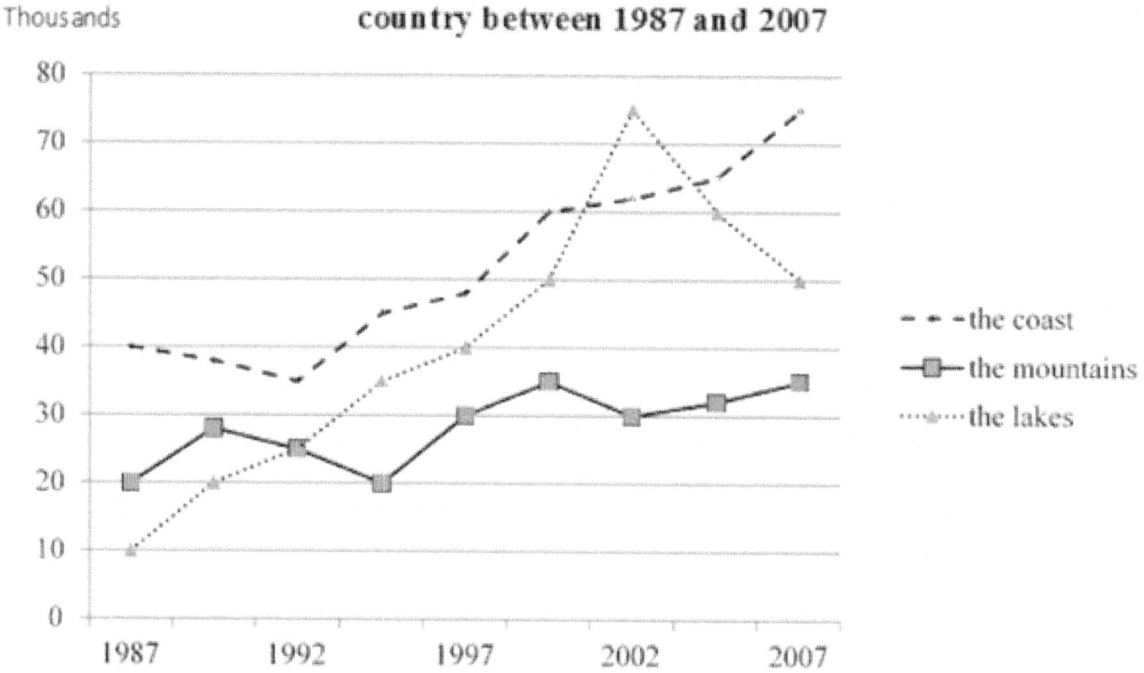

- – – the coast
- —■— the mountains
- ········ the lakes

Power up your Vocabulary

Section B, Unit 11, Lesson 1 - Idiomatic Verbs, New Trends in Business

Vocabulary in Use

In Unit 10 we saw how verbs and adverbs can be combined to describe trends. In this unit we will look at descriptive verbs which have the same function as a verb+ adverb combination. Caution! All of these words have multiple meanings and many can be nouns as well as verbs. In this unit we will learn their use as verbs to describe trends and changes particularly in the fields of business and economics.

Increases

Soar (v) (I) sawr
The action of something rising very quickly like a bird into the sky.
Example
The share prices of electronic payment companies have soared in recent years as consumers have moved towards a cashless economy.

Rocket (v) (I) **rok**-it
The action of something rising dramatically like a rocket blasting off into space.
Example
Investment in warehouses has rocketed recently as e commerce companies try to improve their logistics.

Surge (v) (I) surj
The action of something happening suddenly and with great force like the tide in the oceans.
Example
A surge of migration from Africa into Europe has created new tensions and new business opportunities.

Boom (v) (I) boom
The action of something developing much faster than normal.
Example
Demand for iPhones boomed when the iPhone X was launched.

No change

Stagnate (v) (I) **stag**-neyt
To stop progressing or developing.
Example
Average incomes and consumer spending in the UK have stagnated since the financial crisis in 2008.

Decreases

Collapse (v) (I) k*uh*-**laps**
To fall down, to come to nothing, to fail suddenly and completely, (of a company) to go bankrupt.
Example
A series of retailers such as Toys R Us have collapsed in both Britain and the USA as buyers switch to online shopping.

Dip (v) (T) dip
To decrease **slightly** usually with the implication that the object will **rebound**.
Example
Shares in the supermarket company dipped when the CEO resigned but soon recovered.

Plummet (v) (I) **pluhm**-it
To drop dramatically like a person falling off a cliff.
Example
The number of people using cheques to pay for their shopping has plummeted in recent years.

Plunge (v) (I) (T) pluhnj
A synonym for plummet, to bring something suddenly and forcibly into a condition.
Example
Volkswagen were plunged into a crisis by revelations of cheating in environmental tests on their diesel engines.

Slip (v) (I) slip
To **decline** slightly.
Example
Sales of new cars have slipped a little amid worries about emissions from diesel engines.

Section B, Unit 11, Lesson 2 - Adverbs of Frequency, Shopping

> **What are Adverbs of Frequency?**
>
> Adverbs of frequency tell us how often the action of a verb occurs. You already know some common ones such as always, often, sometimes and never. In this unit we will learn some more academic adverbs of frequency.

Continuously (adv.) k*uh* n-**tin**-yoo-*uh* s-lee
Describes an action which occurs all the time with no breaks.
Example
Amazon has been growing continuously since the 1990s.

Frequently (adv.) **free**-kw*uh* nt-lee
Describes an action which happens often.
Example
Most people shop in convenience stores frequently.

Generally (adv.) **jen**-er-*uh*-lee
Describes an action which usually happens or a statement which is usually true.
Example
Shopping malls are generally located either in city centers or in out of town retail parks.

Occasionally (adv.) *uh*-**key**-zh*uh*-nl-ee
Describes an action which does not occur often.
Example
Most people buy big ticket items such as furniture or cars only occasionally.

Sporadically (adv.) sp*uh*-**rad**-ik-lee
Describes an action which occurs at **ir**regular and **un**predictable intervals.
Example
UK retail sales have been growing only sporadically in the last **decade**.

Power up your Vocabulary

Vocabulary in Use

Many students believe that all adverbs in English end in the suffix …ly. This is a myth. Adverbs can have many other endings. They can also be idiomatic expressions known as adverbials. We will learn some adverbials of frequency on this page.

From time to time (adverbial)   Synonym: sometimes
Example
Research studies of consumers' shopping habits are published from time to time.

Most of the time (adverbial)   Synonym: usually
Example
I buy fast fashion from chain stores most of the time.

Now and again (adverbial)   Synonym: occasionally
Example
But now and again I treat myself to something more up market and exclusive from a boutique.

Once in a while (adverbial)   Synonym: occasionally
Example
I only eat fast food once in a while because it is not good for my health.

When the cows come home (adverbial)   Synonym: never
Example
People who think that traditional high street shopping will revive will be waiting until the cows come home.

Section B, Unit 11, Exercises

Exercise 1: Word Puzzle

Unscramble the letters to make words or phrases from this unit. The first one has been done for you.

1. *iwcnneaoiehl* — *once in a while*
2. raos — …………………………
3. ugplne — …………………………
4. mboo — …………………………
5. lreanglye — …………………………
6. qtfeylurne — …………………………
7. ktocre — …………………………

> **Take it Further**
>
> Find out more about new technology and changes in shopping at our featured retailer
>
> https://www.retaildive.com/news/7-ways-walmart-is-innovating-with-technology/525154/
>
> Make notes of new vocabulary.

Now make the name of a famous global retailer as follows:

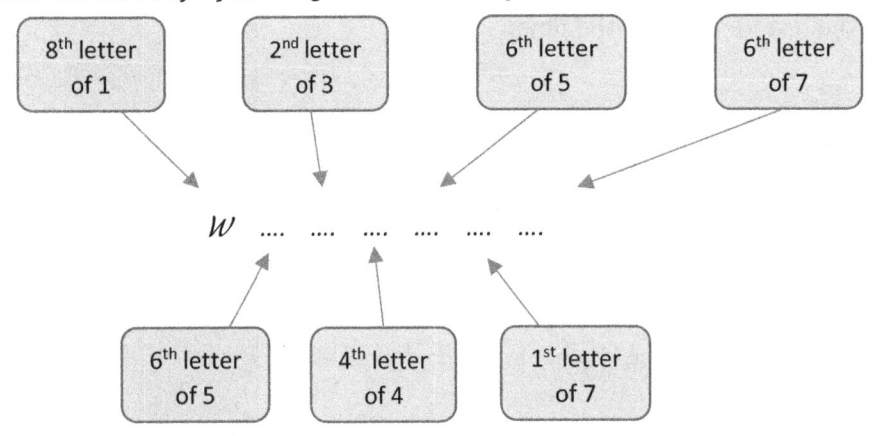

- 8th letter of 1
- 2nd letter of 3
- 6th letter of 5
- 6th letter of 7
- 6th letter of 5
- 4th letter of 4
- 1st letter of 7

w …. …. …. …. …. ….

Exercise 2: Sentence Substitution

Replace the underlined description of a trend with an idiomatic verb. The first one has been done for you.

1. Agricultural production in Zimbabwe ~~fell very quickly~~ *plummeted* in the early part of the 21st century after a botched land reform program.
2. House prices in cities like London and Tokyo have <u>gone up very fast</u> so that many essential workers such as teachers and nurses cannot afford to buy their own homes.
3. The GDP of most European countries <u>did not increase or decrease significantly</u> for several years after the global financial crisis in 2008.

4. The introduction of tariffs caused a <u>slight short-term fall</u> in share prices of some companies which rely on export sales.
5. People who hope for an end to cyber security threats are likely to have to wait <u>for ever</u>.
6. The administrators have announced that talks to save the XYZ fashion chain from <u>bankruptcy and closure</u> have failed.

Exercise 3: Making Sentences

Make sentences using the adverbs about your own shopping habits:

Example
I continuously look for bargains on e- commerce websites.

a)   I sporadically ....
b)   I generally ....
c)   Most of the time I ....
d)   I occasionally ....
e)   Once in a while I ....
f)   I frequently ....

Section B, Unit 12, Lesson 1 - Comment adverbs, the USA

> ### What are Comment Adverbs?
> Adverbs are often used in academic presentations and writing to indicate probability, to comment on, or pass judgement on, statements.
>
> These adverbs can occur at the beginning, in the middle or at the end of a sentence. They have the effect of modifying the meaning of the whole sentence.

Apparently (adv.) *uh*-**par**-*uh* nt-lee
Indicates that you are stating something to be true based on other people's opinions or research not your own.
Example
Apparently, baseball is the second most popular sport in the USA.

Definitely (adv.) **def**-*uh*-nit-lee
Indicates that you are certain about something. Note: definitely is often used for emphasis and does not mean that the statement is really true.
Example
Alaska is definitely the largest state in the USA in terms of land area.

Fortunately (adv.) **fawr**-ch*uh*-nit-lee
Indicates that you think that something is good or lucky.
Example
Fortunately, the Constitution has plenty of checks and balances to limit an elected Officer's ability to do harm.

Frankly (adv.) **frangk**-lee
Indicates that you are stating something even though you know it may be controversial or offend others.
Example
Frankly, I find the rules of football baffling.

Normally (adv.) **nawr**-m*uh*-lee
Indicates that something is true under most circumstances but there may be an exception.
Example
The climate in Florida is normally very pleasant but there is the occasional hurricane.

Vocabulary in Use

Be careful with your punctuation. When comment adverbs are used at the beginning of a sentence they are followed by a comma.

Obviously (adv) ob-vee-*uh* s-lee
Indicates that you are saying something which readers will know but is necessary to introduce the context of what follows.
Example
Obviously, the legacy of civil war continues to shape the culture and politics of modern America.

Presumably (adv) pri-**zoo**-m*uh*-blee
Indicates that you are **inferring** an **assumption** an author has made or a conclusion you are drawing from his/her work.
Example
The Statue of Liberty was a gift from France to the USA, so presumably it is a popular tourist attraction among French visitors to New York.

Regrettably (adv) ri-**gret**-*uh*-b*uh* l-lee
Indicates that you think it would be better if something had not happened.
Example
Regrettably, the symbol of America, the Bald Eagle, is now an endangered species.

Theoretically (adv) thee-*uh*-**ret**-i-k*uh*-lee
Indicates that something is true in theory and often implies that reality may be different.
Example
Theoretically, the United States Constitution is based on a free market economy.

Understandably (adv) uhn-der-**stan**-d*uh*-b*uh*- lee
Indicates that the writer or speaker can understand another person's point of view or action even though they may not agree with it.
Example
Understandably, the United States gave up on the lunar exploration program after the Apollo flights.

Power up your Vocabulary

Section B, Unit 12, Lesson 2 - Adverbs for Perspective and Cohesion

Vocabulary in Use

Adverbs can be used as cohesive devices to link your ideas together or organize your text.

Chronologically (adv.) kron-l-**oj**-i-k*uh* lee
Indicates that events/records are organized according to time when they occurred.
Example
The major periods in the formation of the earth are usually organized chronologically in textbooks.

Consequently (adv.) **kon**-si-kwent-lee
Links cause and effect, indicates that A is the result of B.
Example
Copper conducts electricity very well, consequently it is used to make electrical cables.

Crucially (adv.) **kroo**-sh*uh* lee
Used to stress that a specific point is very important for your whole argument.
Example
Crucially, forensic scientists were able to match DNA left at the scene of the murder over 20 years ago with samples taken when the suspect was arrested for a traffic offense last month.

Respectively (adv.) ri-**spek**-tiv-lee
Indicates that two lists are in the same order.
Example
Hydrogen, Nitrogen and Oxygen have specific densities of 0.09, 1.25 and 1.43 respectively.

Specifically (adv.) spi-**sif**-ik-lee
Indicates that you are going to give more detail, or narrow down a large topic.
Example
There are a lot of greenhouse gases but in this essay, I am going to consider methane specifically.

Word Families

Adverbs are often members of word families. Do not confuse adjectives and adverbs.
Example

| regret (v) (T) | regret (n) (c) | regrettable (adj.) | regrettably (adv.) |

Power up your Vocabulary

> ## Vocabulary in Use
>
> In academic writing it is common to consider a topic from a variety of perspectives. Adverbs can be used to indicate when you are doing this. Note that adverbs used in this way modify the meaning of a whole sentence or sometimes a whole passage. It is important to recognize them while reading.

Environmentally (adv) en-**vahy**-r*uh* n-m*uh* nt-ulee
Modifies a sentence/passage to consider a topic from an environmental perspective.
Example
Environmentally speaking **carbon trading** is nonsense because it does not reduce the total emissions, it just shifts responsibility.

Financially (adv) fi-**nan**-sh*uh* lee,
Modifies a sentence/passage to consider a topic from a point of view related to money.
Example
Developing countries will have to be helped financially to achieve targets for reducing global warming.

Legally (adv) **lee**-g*uh* lee
Modifies a sentence/passage to consider a topic as it relates to the law.
Example
Car manufacturers are legally required to meet emission standards for all new cars.

Personally (adv) **pur**-s*uh*-nl-ee
Modifies a sentence/passage to consider a topic from a personal point of view.
Example
Personally, I think blue is a beautiful color.

Technically (adv) **tek**-ni-k*uh* lee
Modifies a sentence/passage to discuss a technical aspect of the topic.
Example
Technically speaking, much more could be done to clean up rivers and lakes but it is expensive.

Section B, Unit 12, Exercises

Exercise 1: Sentence Completion

Complete the following sentences with a suitable adverb from this unit. The first one has been done for you.

1. I have not researched this personally but *apparently* physics is the least popular subject among secondary school pupils.
2. ……………………….. , something has to be done about climate change but the question is what.
3. According to the WHO the most polluted cities in the world are Kanpur, Faridabad and Gaya, all in India, with PM2.5 concentrations of 173, 172 and 149 …………………………..
4. I know I shouldn't say it, but …………………… the Minister for the Environment is a liar.
5. The history of the Scientific Revolution will be organized ……………………………. starting with the work of Isaac Newton.
6. Finding a way to store electricity **generated** by **solar power** for use later is ……………………… challenging.
7. If the polar icecaps continue to melt at their present rate then …………………….. it will be possible for people to live in the Antarctic at some time in the future.
8. ……………………….. , there were no casualties from yesterday's chemical leak at the Riverside Industrial Estate.

Exercise 2: Word Families

Complete the following table. Use a dictionary if necessary. Number 1 has been done for you.

Verb	Noun	Adjective	Adverb
specify	_____	1. *specific*	specifically
_____	consequence	consequential	2. ………………………….
personify	3. ………………………..	personal	personally
appear	_____	apparent	4. ………………………..
finance	finance	5. ……………………….	financially
theorize	6. ………………………	theoretical	theoretically

Power up your Vocabulary

Exercise 3: Jumbled Syllables

Match phonic syllables from the following jumble to make complete adverbs from this unit. The first one has been done for you.

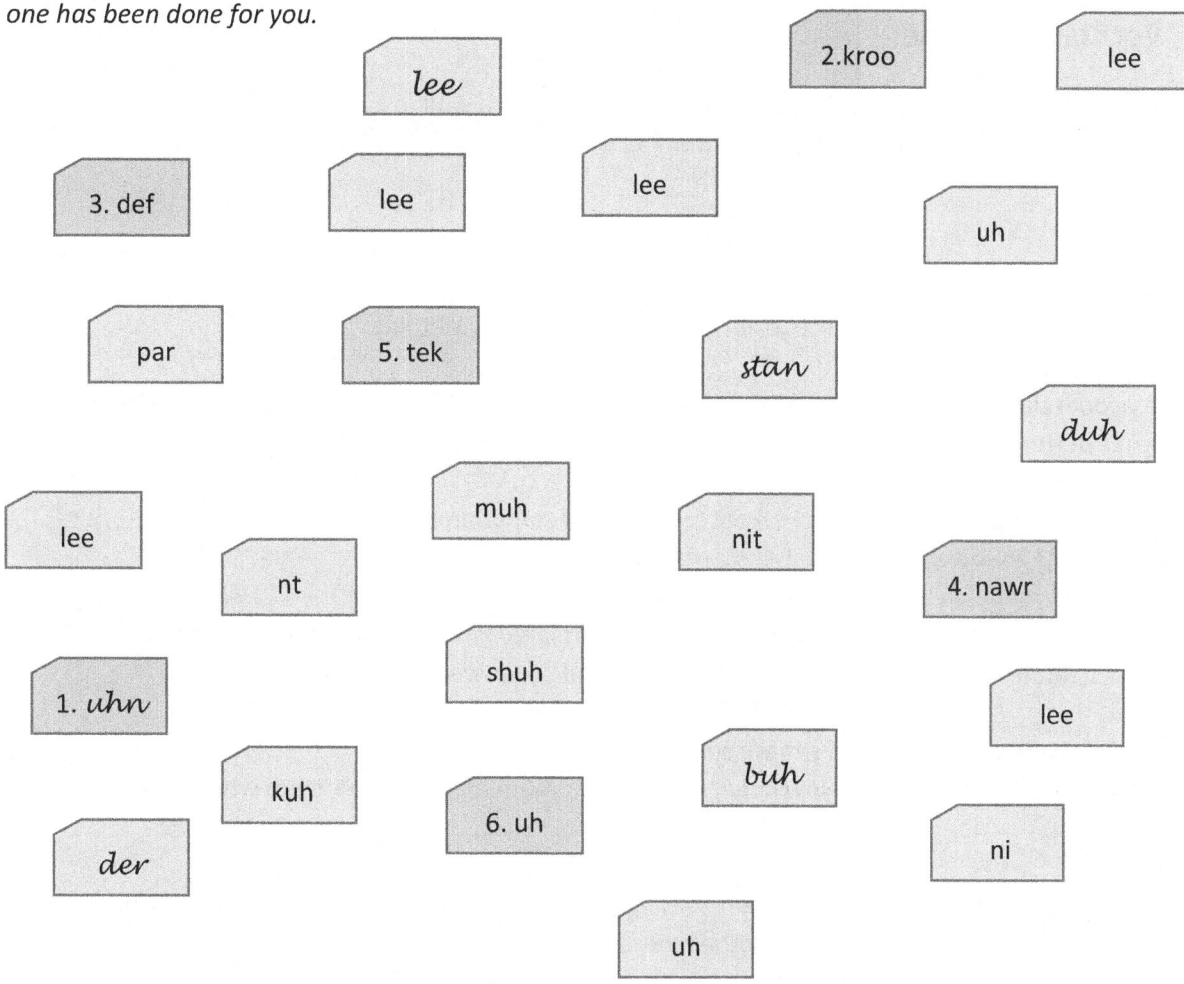

- lee
- 2. kroo
- lee
- 3. def
- lee
- lee
- uh
- par
- 5. tek
- stan
- duh
- lee
- muh
- nit
- nt
- 4. nawr
- shuh
- 1. uhn
- lee
- kuh
- buh
- 6. uh
- ni
- der
- uh

Answers

Phonic spelling	English spelling
1. uhn-der-**stan**-duh-buhlee	understandably
2.	
3.	
4.	
5.	
6.	

Section C, Unit 13, Lesson 1 - Common Mistakes

Vocabulary in Use

Some English words are easily confused because they have similar sounds or spellings but totally different meanings. They come from all the parts of speech we have studied so far.

Affect (v) (T) *uh*-**fekt** To produce a change in something.
Effect (n) (c) ih-**fekt** The result or consequence of something.
Example
Some people claim that computer games have a harmful effect on children's behavior and affect their academic performance in school.

Allusion (n) (c) *uh*-**loo**-zh*uh* n An indirect reference to something in speech or text.
Illusion (n) (c) ih-**loo**-zh*uh* n A false impression of reality.
Example
The police chief made several allusions to recent gang related killings in his statement but said that the media descriptions of a complete breakdown of law and order were an illusion.

Extend (v) (T) ik-**stend** To make something bigger or longer.
Extent (n) (u) ik-**stent** How large, important something is, the degree to which something is true.
Example
The teacher asked the class to what extent they agreed with the use of capital punishment for murder and then extended the topic to include other crimes.

Precede (v) (T) pri-**seed** To go before, to come before.
Proceed (v) (I) pr*uh*-**seed** To go forward usually towards a goal and in an orderly manner.
Example
Months of planning and discussion preceded the decision to proceed with the introduction of an updated smartphone for the Christmas market.

Travel (v) (I) **trav**-*uh* l The action of going to another place on business or on holiday.
Trip (n) (c) trip A journey to another place.
Example
My little sister often gets carsick on trips so we have decided to travel by train next time.

Power up your Vocabulary

> ### Study Tip
>
> In some cases, the confusion between words arises from using the wrong part of speech. This is another reason why it is so important to make notes of parts of speech as you learn new words.

Advice (n) (u) ad-**vahys**   Helpful suggestions given to somebody.
Advise (v) (T) ad-**vahyz**   The action of giving suggestions to somebody.
Example
I asked my careers teacher for some advice about which subjects I should take for my college exams. He advised me to take maths, physics and chemistry.

Confidant (n) (c) **kon**-fi-dahnt   A person you trust and share your worries and secrets with.
Confident (adj) **kon**-fi-d*uh* nt   Having belief in yourself.
Example
I am not a very confident person but it helps a lot when I can discuss my fears with my confidant, Jane, before an important interview or test.

Eminent (adj) **em**-*uh*-n*uh* nt   Describes a person who is famous, and respected in their field.
Imminent (adj) **im**-*uh*-n*uh* nt   Describes something that is about to happen.
Example
Hundreds of people are waiting for the imminent arrival of the eminent historian and TV personality Prof Simon Anderson.

Personal (adj) **pur**-s*uh*-nl   About yourself or something belonging to you.
Personnel (n) (c) **pur**-s*uh*-**nel**   Staff or employees of an organization.
Example
Following reports of thefts from offices, the human resources manager has sent a memo to all personnel reminding them to take care of their personal belongings.

Proponent (n) (c) pr*uh*-**poh**-n*uh* nt   Someone who **puts forward** a policy or agrees with an opinion.
Opponent (n) (c) *uh*-**poh**-n*uh* nt   Someone who disagrees with a policy or an idea.
Example
Proponents of building a third runway at Heathrow airport want construction to start as soon as possible but opponents have vowed to delay construction for as long as possible.

Section C, Unit 13, Lesson 2 - Homonyms

> ### What are Homonyms?
>
> Homonyms are words that sound the same but have different meanings. There are two main types:
>
> **Homographs** are words which have the same spelling but different meanings. They usually have different roots and are sometimes different parts of speech. The pronunciation may also differ.
>
> **Homophones** have different spellings and different meanings but the same or similar pronunciation.

Capital (adj) **kap**-i-tl	Involving death e.g. capital punishment.
Capital (adj), (n) **kap**-i-tl	e.g. capital city, where the government for a country is located.
Capital (n) **kap**-i-tl	(In architecture), the carved stone at the top of a column.
Compliment (n) (c) **kom**-pl*uh*-m*uh*nt	Something nice that you say about another person.
Compliment (v) **kom**-pl*uh*-ment	The action of saying something nice about another person.
Complement (v) **kom**-pl*uh*-ment	Going well together e.g. colors, improving something by adding another element.
Manifest (adj) **man**-*uh*-fest	Describes something which is clear, obvious.
Manifest (v) (itself) **man**-*uh*-fest	The action of something becoming obvious.
Manifest (n) (c) **man**-*uh*-fest	A document used in international trade to list the cargo of a ship or plane.
Sow (v) (I) soh	To plant seeds to grow crops for food.
Sow (n) (c) sou	A female pig.
Spoke (v) spohk	The past tense of speak.
Spoke (n) (c) spohk	Part of a wheel on a bicycle or old car which connects the hub to the rim.

Power up your Vocabulary

Air (n) (u) air	The atmosphere that we breathe in.
Heir (n) (c) air	Someone who inherits money or property when another person dies.
Bail (n) (u) beyl	Money paid by a prisoner to guarantee good behavior in return for being released from custody.
Bail (v) beyl	The action of releasing a prisoner in return for a payment or other conditions guaranteeing good behavior.
Bale (n) (c) beyl	A large bundle of goods e.g. straw, cloth.
Discreet (adj) dih-**skreet**	Describes somebody who is careful to keep secrets.
Discrete (adj) dih-**skreet**	Separate e.g. variables in maths.
Fair (adj) fair	Pale in color e.g. pale skin.
Fair (adj) fair	Equal for all e.g. fair treatment.
Fair (n) (c) fair	A collection of rides and amusements.
Fare (n) (c) fair	The price of a journey e.g. bus fare.
Feat (n) (c) feet	An achievement usually requiring unusual strength or skill.
Feet (n) (plural) feet	The plural of foot.

Study Tips

1. Always make notes of the complete sentence in which you encounter homonyms.

2. When students find two different spellings of a word they often assume that one of the spellings must be wrong. They then use the same spelling for all the meanings of that word. This is a mistake. Always check a dictionary.

Section C, Unit 13, Exercises

Choose the best answer for each of the following questions. The first one has been done for you.

Exercise 1: Multiple Choice

1. (*c*) Which of the following is the best definition of *precede:*
    a) Go ahead with a project
    b) Go backwards
    c) Go before something
    d) Go to another country

2. (   ) Which of the following is not a meaning of *fair*:
    a) Pale e.g. skin
    b) The price of a bus or train ticket
    c) Equal treatment for everybody
    d) A collection of rides and amusements

3. (   ) Which part of speech is *travel*:
    a) A verb
    b) A countable noun
    c) An adjective
    d) An uncountable noun

4. (   ) A *feat* is:
    a) A part of your body at the end of your leg
    b) A measure of length
    c) A goal
    d) A great achievement

5. (   ) Which of the following statements is correct:
    a) A proponent is against a proposal and an opponent supports it
    b) Neither a proponent nor an opponent agrees with a proposal
    c) A proponent is in favor of a proposal and an opponent is against it
    d) Both a proponent and an opponent disagree with a proposal

6. (   ) Something which is about to happen can be described as:
    a) permanent
    b) imminent
    c) eminent
    d) prominent

Power up your Vocabulary

Exercise 2: Find the Mistakes

There is one mistake in each of the following sentences. Correct them. Number 1 is given.

1. My French teacher gave me some advise about improving my listening skills.

   *My French teacher gave me some **advice** about improving my listening skills.*

2. I have applied for an internship and I have an interview with the personal department next week.

   ....

3. My tutor complemented me about the improvement in my maths scores.

   ....

4. Jane is my best friend and confident. I do not know what I would have done without her after my father's accident.

   ....

5. If everyone recycles as much of their trash as possible it can have a big affect on the environment.

   ....

6. The prisoner was granted bale on condition that he surrendered his passport.

   ....

7. The exam question asked "Shakespeare was the greatest English dramatist of all time. To what extend do you agree or disagree with this statement."

   ....

8. Prince Charles will be the air and successor to the present British queen.

   ....

Exercise 3: Anagrams

Unscramble the letters to make words from this unit that are often misused. Write your own definition (s) in your notebook. There may be more than 1.

Example: trdieesc   *discrete*   *An independent variable or something which forms a separate category.*

1. ftamnsei   ....   2. pcaliat   ....   3. kpose   ....
4. slaonlui   ....   5. redcope   ....   6. ltmoencmp   ....

Section C, Unit 14, Review, Units 1-13

- *You will need a pack of ordinary playing cards for this game.*
- *You can play solo, in pairs or in groups.*
- *Shuffle the cards and place the pack face down on your desk or table.*
- *Take the first card from the top of the pack and follow the instructions below.*
- *Say and write the words.*
- *If you can do the activity successfully discard the card. If not put it back on the bottom of the pack and come back to it.*

Example

Ace of hearts = A verb which means to take a trip
--- travel

	Hearts = verbs	Diamonds = adverbs	Spades = nouns	Clubs = adjectives
Ace	A verb which means to take a trip	An adverb which means organized according to time	A noun which begins with the letter Q	An adjective suffix which describes a state of mind.
2	Two verbs which mean to increase very quickly	Two adverbs which can be used to modify extreme adjectives	A noun whose root means two	An adjective beginning with the letter F which has two different meanings
3	Three phrasal verbs with get	Three adverbs which describe the sequence of change	Three nouns with the suffix ...ment	Three negative prefixes beginning with the letter I. Give examples
4	Four words which make a word family with the verb accuse	Four adverbs which describe the increase or decrease of something	Four nouns naming new technologies for cars	Four adjectives which end with the suffix ..ous

5	Five verbs used in critical thinking	Five comment adverbs	Five nouns beginning with the letter T	Five compound adjectives that describe personality
6	Six process verbs	Six adverbs you did not know previously	Six nouns with the suffix .. tion	An adjective with six letters that means very clever.
7	Seven verbs with six letters	Seven adverbs beginning with the letters C and D	Two nouns with Latin roots	Seven letters, can be combined with far to mean hard to believe
8	Eight verbs related to digital business	Any eight adverbs which end in ...ly	A noun with eight letters which means a document in international trade	Eight adjectives beginning with the letter C
9	Nine verbs used to describe a graph	An adverb with nine letters, synonym for usually	Nine nouns naming study skills	A formal synonym for lively with nine letters
10	Ten verbs beginning with the letter D	An adverb which indicates you are sure about an opinion	A noun whose root means ten	Ten adjectives which begin with the letter i
Jack	Define a collocation and give an example	Define a comment adverb and give an example	Define a nominaliser and give an example	Define antonyms and give a pair of examples
Queen	Define a phrasal verb and give an example	Define an adverbial and give an example	Define a suffix and give an example	Define an extreme adjective and give an example
King	Define a word family and give an example	Define an adverb of frequency	Define a compound noun and give an example	Define register and give an example

Section D, Unit 15, Lesson 1 - Maths Vocabulary

Vocabulary in Use

All academic subjects have their own topic specific vocabulary which you need to learn to get the most out of your lessons and textbooks. With maths vocabulary, labelling example diagrams and problems helps a lot.

Review

In Unit 2, Lesson 2 we learned Latin and Greek roots for numbers. These are especially useful in maths. Can you remember the meaning of; **bi, cent, dec, hemi, milli, mono, multi, quad, tri**?

Arithmetic Words

Integer (n) (c) **in**-ti-jer
A whole number, not a **decimal** or fraction.
Example
1,2,3 etc. are integers.

Digit (n) (c) **dij**-it
A symbol used to write numbers.
Example
726 is a three- digit number.

Numerator (n) (c)   **noo**-m*uh*-rey-ter
The number on the top of a fraction.

Denominator (n) (c)   dih-**nom**-*uh*-ney-ter
The number on the bottom of a fraction.

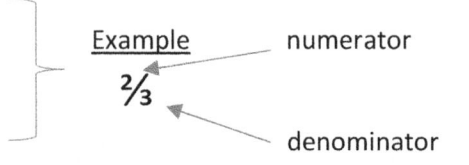

Example $\frac{2}{3}$ — numerator / denominator

Probability (n) (l)
A mathematical expression of the likelihood of an event occurring.
Example
If you toss a coin the probability of it coming down heads is 0.5

Binary numbers (n) (plural)
A number system with only two digits; 0 and 1.
Example
Binary numbers are the basis of all computer operating systems.

Power up your Vocabulary

Algebra Words

Equation (n) (c) ih-**kwey**-sh*uh* n   Root: Equi = equal

an expression or a proposition in algebra stating that two quantities are equal.

Example

x + 5 = 9   is an equation

Constant (n) (c) **kon**-st*uh* nt

In Algebra, a constant is a number on its own, or a letter which stands for a fixed number.

Example

In the equation, x + 5 = 9,   5 and 9 are constants.

Variable (n) (c) **vair**-ee-*uh*-b*uh* l

A quantity that can change within the context of a mathematical problem.

Example

In the equation, x + 2 = 6,   x is the variable.

Formula (n) (c) **fawr**-my*uh*-l*uh*

A rule or principle, frequently expressed in algebraic symbols.

Example

To convert temperatures in **Centigrade** to Fahrenheit use the formula °C x 9/5 + 32 = °F.

Simplify (v) (T) **sim**-pluh-fahy

To make something, such as an equation or a fraction, simpler and easier to understand.

Example

Start with: x = 2w(5wy) then multiply the constants and variables to get $x = 10w^2y$.

Study Tips

Maths vocabulary is cumulative. It pays to take extra time to make sure you understand the basics otherwise you will get lost in more advanced maths.

Maths uses a lot of compound nouns like those we learned in Unit 3. If you already know the simple words on this page use a mathematical dictionary to look up:

simultaneous equations   **differential equations**   **discrete variable**

Section D, Unit 15, Lesson 2 - More Maths Vocabulary

Vocabulary in Use

New roots introduced in this lesson:

circum (Latin) = around   **equ** (Latin) = equal   **hex** (Greek) = six   **semi** (Latin) = half

Geometry Words

Semi-circle (n) (c) **sem**-i-sur-k*uh* |
Half of a circle.
Example
In some cultures, students sit in a semi-circle at the feet of their teacher.

Circumference (n) (c) ser-**kuhm**-fer-*uh* ns
The distance around the outside of a circle.
Example
The circumference of the earth is 40,075 kilometers.

Equilateral triangle (n) (c) ee-kw*uh*-**lat**-er-*uh* | **trahy**-ang-g*uh* |
A triangle with three sides of equal length and three equal angles of 60 degrees.
Example
The theory of equilateral triangles was developed by the ancient Greek mathematician Euclid.

Isosceles triangle (n) (c) ahy-**sos**-*uh*-leez **trahy**-ang-g*uh* |
A triangle with two equal sides and two equal angles.
Example
Nobody knows who first discovered the theory of the Isosceles triangle in ancient Greece.

Hexagon (n) (c) **hek**-s*uh*-gon
In geometry, a two-dimensional shape with six sides.
Example
The logo used on BMW cars is a blue and white hexagon.

Power up your Vocabulary

Vocabulary in Use

Nowadays, nearly all academic subjects require knowledge of applied maths and statistics. These topics too have their own specialist vocabulary. Here are some terms you will find useful.

Mean (n) (c) meen
The average result obtained from a test, survey, or experiment, usually a number.
Example
A survey shows that the mean height of adults in the UK is 178.6cm for men and 163.7cm for women.

Median (n) (c) **mee**-dee-*uh* n
The value in a set of results that divides them in half – the middle value.
Example
In the 2016-17 tax year the median salary in the US was $46,500.

Mode (n) (c) mohd
The most frequently occurring value in a test, survey, or experiment.
Example
In a class survey of how often students changed their smartphones, the mode was every nine months.

> **Study Tip**
>
> A lot of words in maths have different meanings in everyday speech and can be different parts of speech e.g. mean
>
> Mean (n) (c) the average of a set of results
>
> Mean (adj) selfish with money
>
> Mean (v) to have in mind, intend, express something
>
> Use a specialist maths dictionary to find the correct meaning in maths.

Standard deviation (sd) (n) (c) **stan**-derd dee-vee-**ey**-sh*uh* n
The Standard Deviation is a measure of how spread out numbers are calculated as the square root of the variance where the variance is the average of the squared differences from the mean.
Example
Survey results can be considered reliable if 95% of the results are within + or – 1 standard deviation of the mean.

Correlation coefficient (n) (c) kawr-*uh*-**ley**-sh*uh* n koh-*uh*-**fish**-*uh* nt
A measure of the interdependence of two random variables that ranges in value from -1 to +1.
Example
The closer a correlation coefficient is to 1 the closer the relationship between the variables.

Section D, Unit 15, Exercises

Exercise 1: Word Puzzle

Unscramble the words from this unit in the puzzle below. Then use the numbered letters to make the name of a famous ancient Greek mathematician. Who was he?

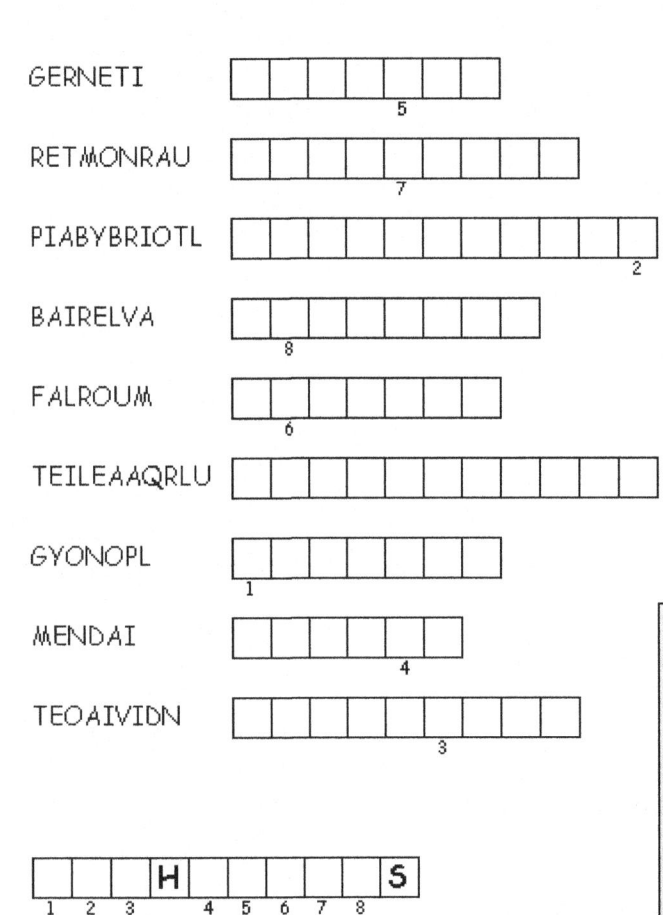

GERNETI — ⬜⬜⬜⬜⬜⬜⬜ (5)

RETMONRAU — ⬜⬜⬜⬜⬜⬜⬜⬜⬜ (7)

PIABYBRIOTL — ⬜⬜⬜⬜⬜⬜⬜⬜⬜⬜⬜ (2)

BAIRELVA — ⬜⬜⬜⬜⬜⬜⬜⬜ (8)

FALROUM — ⬜⬜⬜⬜⬜⬜⬜ (6)

TEILEAAQRLU — ⬜⬜⬜⬜⬜⬜⬜⬜⬜⬜⬜

GYONOPL — ⬜⬜⬜⬜⬜⬜⬜ (1)

MENDAI — ⬜⬜⬜⬜⬜⬜ (4)

TEOAIVIDN — ⬜⬜⬜⬜⬜⬜⬜⬜⬜ (3)

⬜ ⬜ ⬜ H ⬜ ⬜ ⬜ S
1 2 3 4 5 6 7 8

Take it Further

A lot of the geometry in these pages, and much else in mathematics, stems from the work of the ancient Greek mathematicians. To find out more about two of them click:

https://www.biographyonline.net/scientists/euclid.html

https://www.famousscientists.org/pythagoras/

Power up your Vocabulary

Exercise 2: Complete the Questions

Complete the questions in a simple maths test with words from Unit 15. The first one has been done for you.

1. The following fraction has been simplified. What was the original *denominator*?

$$\frac{16}{\cancel{xxxxx}} = \frac{1}{2}$$ *(The answer is 32)*

2. If the triangle below has sides (a) and (b) each of 5cms and side (c) of 7cms we can say the triangle is an ……………………….. triangle.

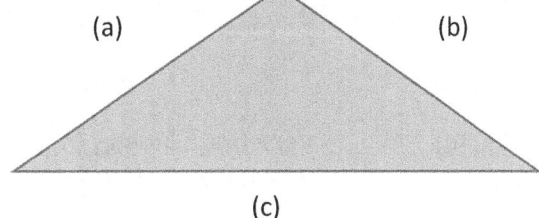

3. In a class survey, students were asked how many books they had read in the past month. The answers are given below. The number 3 is the ………………… in this range.

10, 3, 5, 3, 3, 2, 0, 4, 3, 5, 3, 1, 3, 3, 8

4. 1582 is a four ………………… number.

5. The formula C = $2\pi r$ can be used to calculate the ……………………………… of a circle.

6. A letter which stands for a fixed number in algebra is called a ………………………………

7. In a medical experiment two variables had a strong relationship of 0.81. The mathematical term for this value is a ……………………….. ……………………….

8. In geometry the shape below can be described as a ………………………………

9. A line of computer code 0011010101110111 uses …………………………. numbers.

Exercise 3: Word Finder

How many maths words can you make from the following compound:

SIMULTANEOUS EQUATIONS

Example: *sum*

Use words from this unit and others you know. You have five minutes.

Power up your Vocabulary

Section D, Unit 16, Lesson 1 - Science Vocabulary

> **Study Tip**
>
> Science has a huge and growing vocabulary. One way to manage your learning is by **classification**. Compound nouns, Latin and Greek roots and prefixes such as we have learned can all help you do this. In this lesson we will look at some examples and add some new roots to our collection.

--- Biology ---

Marine biology (n) (u) **Vertebrate biology** (n) (u) **Invertebrate biology** (n) (u)
m*uh*-**reen** bahy-**ol**-*uh*-jee   **vur**-t*uh*-brit bahy-**ol**-*uh*-jee   in-**vur**-t*uh*-brit bahy-**ol**-*uh*-jee

Root: **mar** (Latin) = sea   Root: **vertebra** (Latin) = joint

The study of sea creatures.   The study of creatures with   The study of creatures without a
                              a backbone.   backbone.

Examples

Rachel Carson, founder of the modern environmental movement, studied marine biology.

Vertebrate biology includes the study of creatures including humans, other mammals, fish and amphibians such as crocodiles which all have a spine or backbone.

Some students do not like studying invertebrate biology because they think these creatures are scary creepy crawlies.

--- Subjects related to biology ---

Zoology (n) (u) zoh-**ol**-*uh*-jee   **bioengineering** (n) (u) bahy-oh-en-j*uh*-**neer**-ing

The study of animals.   The application of engineering principles, methods,
                                              and technology to the fields of biology and medicine.

Examples

Zoology is becoming increasingly important as more and more species are facing extinction in the wild.

The discovery of DNA means that bioengineering is now the most promising source of new drugs.

Power up your Vocabulary

> ## Review
>
> In Unit 7 we looked at verbs which describe the action of a process. Some of these are useful to describe processes you will be asked to study in lab experiments or science classes.
> Can you remember the meaning and collocations of?
>
> > drill   enrich   filter out   generate   harvest   incinerate
>
> On this page we will learn some more process verbs.

Decompose (v) (T) dee-k*uh* m-**pohz**
The process of something breaking down into its constituent parts.
Example
Some domestic waste, such as vegetables, will decompose naturally and so poses no threat to the environment.

Dissect (v) (T) dih-**sekt**
To cut something apart and examine each part in detail.
Example
One of the first things students learn in biology classes is to dissect creatures such as frogs.

Distill (v) (T) dih-**stil**
The process of evaporating and then cooling a substance to collect the drops of pure liquid that condense.
Example
Scotland is famous for distilling whisky.

Ferment (v) (I) **fur**-ment
The process of leaving something in the sun until the action of yeast or bacteria turns it to alcohol.
Example
If you leave a banana in a hot room for a week it will ferment.

Germinate (v) (I) **jur**-m*uh*-neyt
The process of something beginning to grow from a seed.
Example
Botanists study how seeds germinate to become fully grown plants.

Power up your Vocabulary

Section D, Unit 16, Lesson 2 - More Science Vocabulary

Vocabulary in Use

In Unit 3 Lesson 2 we looked at the way in which compound nouns can be used to name new products and new technologies. The same principle is applied in science. Sometimes these new words become very fashionable. They are then called **buzz words**. Even though they are very modern ideas a lot of buzz words still use ancient Latin and Greek roots.

Ecosystem (n) (c) **ek**-oh-sis-t*uh* m   Root: **eco** (Greek) = house

A set of interconnected elements, formed by the interaction of a community of organisms with their environment.

Example

In most western countries land developers have to prepare a report which assesses the impact of their project on the local ecosystem.

Ergonomics (n) (u) ur-g*uh*-**nom**-iks   Root: **erg** (Greek) = work

The study of the interface between humans and machines or buildings.

Example

Ergonomics is increasingly important in the design of many modern products such as cars.

Genetic engineering (n) (u) j*uh*-**net**-ik en-j*uh*-**neer**-ing   Root: **gen** (Greek) = birth

Making scientific changes to genetic material to alter cells or grow new organisms.

Example

Advances in genetic engineering may allow scientists in the future to grow new human organs to replace diseased ones.

Nano technology (n) (I) **nan**-oh tek-**nol**-*uh*-jee   Root: **nanos** (Greek) = dwarf

Technologies which use materials at the nano (one-billionth of a meter) level of size.

Example

Coatings using materials made with nano technology can improve lubrication and reduce friction in car engines thus making them more efficient.

Polymer (n) (c) **pol**-*uh*-mer   Root: **poly** (Greek) = many

A chemical compound made by combining many molecules.

Examples

A lot of polymers, especially plastics, do not **decompose** naturally and are very difficult to recycle, so they cause a lot of damage to the environment.

Power up your Vocabulary

Vocabulary in Use

The basis of all physics, chemistry and biology classes in high school is the scientific process. On this page we will learn some vocabulary associated with it.

Review

In Unit 1 and Unit 8 we looked at some nouns and verbs used in science education. Can you remember the meaning of; **dissertation, experiment, hypothesize?**

Objective (n) (c) *uh* b-**jek**-tiv
The aim or goal of a research project.
Example
The objective of a research project is often to test whether a **hypothesis** is true.

Prediction (n) (c) pri-**dik**-sh*uh* n
A statement about something which is expected to happen.
Example
Climate scientists are currently making a lot of predictions about the effects of global warming.

Precision (n) (u) pri-**sizh**-*uh* n
The degree of accuracy of a statement or a set of results.
Example
In science course work, the **assignment** instructions will often tell you the degree of precision required in your answer e.g. 2 **decimal** places.

Repeatable (adj.) ri-**peetey**-b*uh* l
The quality of being able to repeat something and get the same answer.
Example
The results of all research in a scientific **dissertation** should be repeatable.

Anomaly (n) (c) *uh*-**nom**-*uh*-lee
Something in a set of results which does not fit the expected or observed pattern.
Example
If there are a lot of anomalies in the results of an **experiment** then either the hypothesis was wrong or the experiment was not carried out correctly.

Power up your Vocabulary

Section D, Unit 16, Exercises

Exercise 1: Spidergrams

Complete the following diagram with words from this unit. The first one has been done for you.

> **Study Tip**
>
> Classifying and grouping new words in different ways will give you fresh insights into their meaning and usage.

1. Prefixes, de..., re....... — decompose, repeatable

2. Greek roots
   - ....
   - ....
   - ....
   - ....

3. Academic subjects in science
   - a) ....
   - b) ....
   - c) ....
   - d) ....
   - e) ....
   - f) ....

4. Aspects of the scientific process
   - a) ....
   - b) ....
   - c) ....
   - d) ....
   - e) ....

5. Process verbs
   - a) ....
   - b) ....
   - c) ....
   - d) ....
   - e) ....

Power up your Vocabulary

Exercise 2: Sentence Completion

*Complete the following definition sentences with words from the word bank. The first letters of each answer form the name of a **renowned** Scottish scientist. Who was he?*

1. When grapes are left out in the sun to turn into alcohol they ………………………

2. ……………………….. is used to design desks, chairs and computer which are safer, healthier and more comfortable to use.

3. If you study ……………………….. you may research the lifecycles of fish in the sea.

4. The branch of biology which studies insects and other creatures without a backbone is called …………………….. ……………………

5 …………… ……………………….. is a branch of science which develops applications for a range of materials that are only one molecule thick.

6. Gardeners often put seeds in a warm, dark place in the spring to ……………………. and grow into plants and flowers in the summer.

The name of a famous Scottish scientist:

Alexander --- L --- --- --- --- ---

Word Bank	
ergonomics	germinate
marine biology	nano technology
ferment	invertebrate biology

Power up your Vocabulary

Exercise 3: Classification

*The academic subjects we have learned in this unit are sometimes collectively called the **life sciences**. Classify the following pictures in the most appropriate branch of the life sciences. The first category has been done for you.*

```
                        Life sciences
         ┌───────────────┬───────────────┬───────────────┐
  vertebrate biology  invertebrate biology  marine biology   bioengineering
         c              ……………….           ……………….          ……………….
         h              ……………….           ……………….          ……………….
```

a)

b)

c)

d)

e)

f)

g)

h)

Power up your Vocabulary

Section D, Unit 17, Lesson 1 - IT Vocabulary

> ### Vocabulary in Use
>
> As you move through secondary school you will need to use computers to study as well as for fun and games. In this lesson we will learn some of the vocabulary you will need to do this. We will start with hardware before moving on to software, new concepts in IT and finally some of the issues arising from the use of IT in education and work.

Additive Printer (n) (c) **ad**-i-tiv **prin**-ter
A device which takes instructions from a computer to make objects by printing layers of tiny particles. (Also known as 3D printer)
Example
It is already possible to print an entire house in a few days using an additive printer.

CAD/CAM (n) (u) **kad**-kam
Abbreviation for a combination of computer aided manufacturing and computer aided design.
Example
CAD/CAM systems allow a company to design as well as manufacture a product.

Graphical user interface (GUI) (n) (c) **graf**-ik-ul **yoo**-zer **in**-ter-feys
Part of a computer which allows the use of diagrams, graphs etc. as well as standard text.
Example
Introduction of user friendly GUI meant that a lot more people could work on a computer.

Network (n) (c) **net**-wurk
In computing, a system of servers, terminals, printers etc. which are digitally connected by cables and hardware to communicate with each other.
Example
Schools, offices and factories rely on networks to enable people to work together using computers.

Router (n) (c) **rou**-ter
Hardware which decides the best way for data to be sent to its destination in a computer network.
Example
The new 5G cell phone systems rely on a new generation of routers which use bandwidth much more efficiently to make applications run faster.

Power up your Vocabulary

> **Study Tip**
>
> A lot of IT vocabulary uses abbreviations such as **GUI, CAD/CAM and ISP**. Don't just copy or memorise them, make sure you know what they mean.

Algorithm (n) (c) **al**-g*uh*-ri*th*-*uh* m
A step-by-step procedure for solving a problem or accomplishing an end e.g. to ranks websites for each keyword or combination of keywords.
Examples
Companies such as Google and Facebook are under a lot of pressure to change their algorithms to stop users seeing 'hate' related websites.

Blockchain (n) (u) blokcheyn
A software database of transactions in cryptocurrencies such as Bitcoin.
Example
Blockchain software is spreading rapidly throughout the banking system as the world moves towards a cashless economy.

Database (n) (c) **dey**-t*uh*-beys
Software which collects and classifies huge amounts of a data to make it easy to search.
Example
Libraries use databases to help students find books and papers relevant to their academic projects.

Internet Service Provider (ISP) (n) (c) **in**-ter-net **sur**-vis pr*uh*-**vahy**-der
Companies which provide subscribers access to the internet.
Example
ISP providers in many countries are subject to monitoring by government agencies.

Spreadsheet (n) (c) **spred**-sheet
Software in which data is arranged in the rows and columns of a grid and can be manipulated and used in calculations.
Example
Learning how to use spreadsheets such as Excel is a vital skill for business and accountancy students.

Power up your Vocabulary

Section D, Unit 17, Lesson 2 - More IT Vocabulary

New Developments in IT

Beta testing (n) (u) **bee**-t*uh* testing
In IT, the second stage of testing a new piece of software or game usually carried out by customers in return for a discount price or early access to the product.
Example
Beta testing allows companies to get feedback from customers before finalising a design.

Cloud computing (n) (u) kloud k*uh* m-**pyoo**-ting
A business model which allows organizations to buy space on huge servers owned by another company to store data instead of keeping it in their facilities.
Example
Cloud computing providers such as Amazon claim that the service is cheaper for small businesses and requires less technical knowledge than managing their data themselves.

Co-creation (n) (u) **ko**-kree-**ey**-sh*uh* n
The process of adding content or value to something by customers and suppliers working together.
Example
Some fashion brands now use co-creation to encourage consumers to help design clothes they would like to buy using social media.

(The) internet of things (n) (u) **in**-ter-net uv thingz
A system in which domestic appliances, tools etc. are digitally connected to the internet and can be controlled or monitored remotely.
Example
The internet of things allows people to switch their home heating or air conditioning on or off from their office or car via their smartphone.

(The) knowledge economy (n) (c) **nol**-ij ih-**kon**-*uh*-mee
An economic model in which a country focuses on producing goods or services which require advanced IT based knowledge, rather than labor, to make or operate.
Example
Most western countries are rapidly becoming knowledge economies and this is changing the skill set required in the workforce.

Power up your Vocabulary

> ## Review
>
> In Unit 3 Lesson 1 we learned that several compound nouns can be formed from the same base word. Can you remember some examples formed from carbon? In this lesson we will see the same pattern with **cyber.** Remember to pay attention to punctuation and think about how you can best learn families of compounds.

Cybercrime (n) (u) **sahy**-ber-krahym
Criminal behavior online including fraud and selling fake or dangerous goods.
Example
The annual cost of cybercrime is estimated to be over $100 billion.

Cyber-espionage (n) (u) **sahy**-ber-**es**-pee-*uh*-nahzh
The use of the internet to spy on or steal information from companies or countries.
Example
Cyber espionage is increasingly being used to steal business secrets and technology.

Cyber-security (n) (u) **sahy**-ber-si-**ky*oo*** r-i-tee
Hardware and software designed to protect computer systems and users and prevent cybercrime and espionage.
Example
Virus protection programs and passwords are common examples of cyber security.

(the) Digital divide (n) (u) **dij**-i-tl dih-**vahyd**
The differences in lifestyle and opportunities between people who have access to the internet and computer skills and those who do not.
Example
The digital divide is a serious problem in education and tends to disadvantage children from poor families.

Connectivity (n) (u) kon-ek-**tiv**-i-tee
A measure of the proportion of a population who are connected to the internet via computers or smartphones.
Example
South Korea has the highest connectivity rate in the world.

Section D, Unit 17, Exercises

Exercise 1: Dialogue

Complete the following dialogue with words from this unit. Two teachers are discussing what should be in the curriculum for a school's IT courses. Use the word bank. The first one has been done for you.

Word Bank

blockchain	digital divide	*cyber security*
databases	algorithms	internet of things
spreadsheets		internet Service Providers

Teacher A: There is just not enough weeks in the term to cover everything, so what do you think should be our priorities?

Teacher B: It's like the wild west out there on the internet, so, no question, it has be to be safety.

Teacher A: You mean we focus on (1) *cyber security*; teach the kids how to stay safe on line?

Teacher B: Absolutely.

Teacher A: OK but that is not enough. I keep hearing from colleagues that too many students can't use formulas in (2) ……………………. to do calculations in applied maths and can't use (3) …………….. to find resources for projects in history and geography.

Teacher B: **Theoretically** yes. But it is not so easy. 45-minute periods are too short to give them much practice and some of the kids from poorer families don't have computers at home to practice. There is a real (4) ……………… ………………. in this school which worries me.

Teacher A: I know. I am trying to get funds to set up an afterschool computer club. We have approached some of the big (5) …………………. ……………………… ……………………. like BT and they seem interested in donating cash or equipment.

Teacher B: That would be great. So, it's safety and online study skills. Then what?

Teacher A: By the time these kids are ready for work a lot of what we are teaching now in IT will be out of date. There is so much new stuff happening, I want to develop a module ….

Teacher B: What new stuff have you got in mind?

Power up your Vocabulary

Teacher A: Well (6) …………………… for a start. That is where the banking and finance industries are going. There will be plenty of jobs. Then I was talking to ABC Plant the other day. They make tools for the building industry. They want to connect them to the (7) …………………… …. ………………… but they can't find programmers to write the code. It is mostly (8) …………………… to help the machines learn the rules and search their own databases for the right actions to take. We should do something with the basic maths involved.

Teacher B: Sounds good and it is more than enough for a term.

Exercise 2: Find the IT Phrase

Unscramble the letters to find words from this unit. Put the numbered letters in the box below to find the name of a place associated with IT. Where is it?

a) ERROTU

b) VETADDII TEPRINR

c) TERNKWO

d) TEAB TEGTINS

e) CO-TONCAIRE

f) NELKOGDEW MOYCENO

g) REBCY SOEGAIPEN

h) NYCNIVCOTETI

Exercise 3: Word String

How many compound nouns and abbreviations from this unit can you find in the word string below? The first one has been done for you.

ISPcloudcomputinggraphicaluserinterfacecyberespionageinternetofthingsCADCAMadditiveprinter

Answers

ISP ....

....

Power up your Vocabulary

Section D, Unit 18, Lesson 1 - Environmental Science Vocabulary

Review

In Unit 2 we learned some environmental science words using the root **bio**. Can you remember the meaning of **biomass and biodegradable**?
In Unit 3 we learned **greenhouse gases**. Can you remember what effect they have on the environment?

Vocabulary in Use

In Unit 1 we met some common noun suffixes. In this unit we will add:

…ant/ent a substance which does something.
…. cide about killing something

Pollutant (n) (c) p*uh*-**loot**-nt
A collective noun for substances which cause pollution.
Example
Rivers often contain a huge range of different pollutants which makes cleaning them difficult.

Effluent (n) (l) **ef**-loo-*uh* nt
Pollutants, usually in liquid form, which flow into rivers, lakes or the sea.
Example
Most countries fine farmers and factories which discharge effluents, but the practice continues.

Heavy metal (n) (c) **hev**-ee **met**-l
A group of elements of high density including mercury and cadmium.
Example
Heavy metals often sank into the ground underneath old factories. They are highly toxic and are not **biodegradable**. This makes it difficult to reuse the old sites.

Pesticide (n) (c) **pes**-t*uh*-sahyd
Chemicals intended to kill insects or small animals which damage farmers' crops.
Example
When too much pesticide is used it can also kill plants and trees and pollute the soil and water.

Particulate matter (PM) (n) (u) per-**tik**-y*uh*-lit **mat**-er
Tiny pieces of solid material suspended in gases.
Example
The most dangerous particulate matter is PM2.5 emitted from car exhausts.

Issues in Environmental Science

Review

In Unit 6 we learned some common negative prefixes for adjectives. How many can you remember?

Vocabulary in Use

Negative prefixes can also be used with nouns. New noun prefixes introduced in this unit:
De.........   removal of something
Over......   too much of something

Deforestation (n) (u) dee-**fawr**-ist-a-sh*uh* n
The process of cutting down and not replacing trees.
Example
Large scale deforestation in the Amazon jungle reduces the world's capacity to absorb Carbon dioxide.

Desertification (n) (u) dih-zur-t*uh*-fi-**key**-sh*uh* n
The process of once fertile regions drying up, suffering soil erosion and turning to desert.
Example
Desertification in Central Asia leads to annual dust storms in Beijing.

Habitat destruction (n) (u) **hab**-i-tat dih-**struhk**-sh*uh* n
The process of human occupation and development of wild areas where animals and plants live.
Example
Habitat destruction means that many species are left with nowhere to live and they eventually become extinct.

Over fishing (n) (u) **oh**-ver **fish**-ing
The practice of catching too much fish from the oceans which does not allow time for stocks to recover.
Example
The EU has tried to prevent over fishing by imposing quotas on the amount of fish that each country can catch.

Salinity (n) (u) **sey**-leen-ity
The amount of salts in the soil.
Example
Irrigation projects such as the Aswan Dam in Egypt can cause levels of salinity to rise which makes the soil less fertile.

Power up your Vocabulary

Section D, Unit 18, Lesson 2 - More Environmental Science Vocabulary

Measurements and Techniques

Carbon Dating (n) (u) **kahr**-b*uh* n deyting
A method of calculating the age of organic items by using Carbon 14 deposits.
Example
Carbon dating can be very useful for studying the history of climate and environment.

Concentration (n) (l) kon-s*uh* n-**trey**-sh*uh* n
(In environmental science) A measure of how much of one substance is contained in a given volume of another substance, often expressed as parts per million (ppm).
Example
High concentrations of particulate matter (PM) in the air lead to high levels of diseases such as asthma.

Frequency (n) (l) **free**-kw*uh* n-see
(In environmental science) A measure of how often something happens.
Example
The frequency of extreme weather events such as heatwaves and droughts seem to be increasing, perhaps as a result of climate change.

Incidence (n) (u) **in**-si-d*uh* ns
A measure of how common something is in a given population.
Example
Doctors study the incidence of diseases caused by various pollutants such as **heavy metals,** often expressed as x cases per 100,000 people.

Sampling (n) (u) **sam**-pling
A research technique which uses a few examples to **infer** conclusions about a large population.
Examples
When using sampling techniques, it is very important to choose samples which are representative of the whole population.

> ### Study Tip
>
> Many of these words have other meanings in general use, or other branches of science. Compare concentration in this unit with the same word in Unit 1. Always, note the context when learning new words.

Power up your Vocabulary

Solutions

Conservation (n) (u) kon-ser-**vey**-sh*uh* n
The practice of protecting and preserving something usually involving laws or government supervision.
Example
Conservation can protect natural habitats from destruction and ensure plants and animals have suitable places to live.

Organic farming (n) (u) awr-**gan**-ik **fahr**-ming
A method of growing food or feeding farm animals using only natural products and no chemical fertilizers or pesticides.
Example
Animal rights supporters say organic farming is less cruel to animals and also benefits the environment.

Regeneration (n) (u) ri-jen-*uh*-**rey**-sh*uh* n
The process of bringing new life to something.
Example
Part of the legacy of the London Olympics was the regeneration of a poor and polluted area of East London.

Substitution (n) (l) **suhb**-sti-tyoo-shuhn
The replacement of one thing by another.
Example
Bags made from natural fibers can be substituted for plastic bags resulting in less ocean pollution.

Sustainable development (n) (l) s*uh*-**stey**-n*uh*-b*uh* l dih-**vel**-*uh* p-m*uh* nt
The process of meeting the needs of the present generation without depleting the earth's resources or harming the environment for future generations.
Example
Many countries now regard sustainable development as their goal but achieving it is not easy.

Study Tip

As we saw in Unit 1 nominalisers like the ones in this unit have word families and should be learned that way.

Example

Conserve (v)   Conservation (n) (c)   Conservationist (n) (c) (person)   Conserved (adj)

Power up your Vocabulary

Section D, Unit 18, Exercises

Exercise 1: Multiple Choice, definitions and Usage

Choose the best answer for each of the following questions. The first one has been done for you.

1. (*d*) Which of the following is the best definition of conservation:
   a) Redevelopment of a run- down area.   b) How often bad weather occurs.
   c) Economic growth which does not harm the environment.
   d) *Keeping a natural habitat unspoilt so that animals and plants can go on living there.*

2. (   ) Deforestation is a major environmental concern in which area:
   a) The Antarctic   b) The Amazon jungle
   c) Everywhere   d) Egypt

3. (   ) Statistics about the concentration of PM 2.5 in the air measure:
   a) The age of the particles.   b) The number of particles per million
   c) The size of the particles   d) The source of the particles

4. (   ) The prefix over…… means:
   a) Too much of something   b) Not enough of something
   c) A lot of something   d) None of the above

5. (   ) Effluent is a particular type of pollution which is distinctive because it is:
   a) gas   b) liquid
   c) smelly   d) solid

6. (   ) Which of the following words forms a compound with carbon to name a process use to find out the age of something:
   a) capture   b) trading
   c) zero   d) dating

7. (   ) Which of the following is the best definition of sampling as a research technique:
   a) All of the statements below   b) Using all of the population
   c) Using random samples of the population   d) Using representative examples of a population.

8. (   ) Salinity refers to the amount of what in the soil:
   a) water   b) heavy metals
   c) salts   d) acid

Power up your Vocabulary

Exercise 2: Complete a Factsheet

In the UK developers wishing to carry out a major project have to complete an environmental impact assessment (EIA) before they are allowed to start work. They are long and complicated documents. But local newspapers often summarise the key points in a fact sheet. Complete the following fact sheet about a proposed urban ring road for city Z using words from the word bank below. Number 1 has been done for you.

Word Bank

sampling	regeneration	deforestation
organic farm	habitat destruction	sustainable
Incidence	carbon dating	

The Good News

- The ring road project includes a (1) *regeneration* plan which will bring $300 million of investment and new homes, shops and businesses to one of the most run-down parts of the city. That is surely welcome.
- There will be two electric vehicle **charging stations** along the route. Transport groups have welcomed this as a step towards (2) .... development.
- The project includes cycle lanes and pedestrian subways as well as vehicle roads. It is claimed this will reduce the (3) .... of deaths and injuries among cyclists and pedestrians by 50%.
- Archaeologists at the City University have been granted time and money before construction starts to excavate the site found at Queen Victoria Street during preliminary surveys. The results of (4) .... suggest the site could contain an important **prehistoric** burial ground.

The Bad News

- The planners have chosen the northern route which goes through Bluebell wood. This will involve the loss of 2.5 acres of woodland. People think of (5) .... as a third world problem. But it is going to happen here unless the Save Our Woods Campaign can reverse this decision.
- It is not only the trees which will be lost. (6) .... will also threaten the extinction of two unique species of butterflies which currently live in Bluebell wood.

Power up your Vocabulary

- If that were not enough the proposed route will also destroy the city's only (7) …………… ………..and the farmer's market which it supplies. That means no more vegetables free of pesticides.

Our (8) ………………….. Suggests that public opinion is split 50:50 about whether all this is a price worth paying to ease the city's traffic problems. Tell us what you think.

Exercise 3: Word Search

Find the words in the puzzle. Words may be horizontal, vertical or diagonal. Spellings may be forwards or backwards. One example has been highlighted for you.

Environmental Science

```
b c f r e q u e n c y m j t i
f y e q p r r q k c j y o s n
s u b s t i t u t i o n f i c
p t d f s n v e h w a i w n i
q n w e u i j g f d s v m o d
p a w g s r y h q h v z y i e
r t v w t t w s i t h j e t n
w u h u a o r n j v f d m a c
h l i l i a g u h s i l u v e
x l l p n h w m c c c l t r b
n o i t a c i f i t r e s e d
u p f x b h f t s m i r u s d
a v j n l w s s f e t o z n y
c s b a e e c g a s q d n o j
t n e m p o l e v e d b y c o
```

conservationist   desertification   destruction   development
fishing   frequency   incidence   pesticide
pollutant   substitution   sustainable

Power up your Vocabulary

Section D, Unit 19, Lesson 1 - Historical Vocabulary

Vocabulary in Use

On this page we will continue to explore prefixes. So far, we have looked at negative prefixes. But not all prefixes make a word negative. Some prefixes used with adjectives indicate time and are useful in history:

Pre……. before something   **Post** ….. after something

Review

Can you remember?
- How many years in a decade, a century?
- What do the adverbs; **previously, subsequently, simultaneously** mean?

Prehistoric (adj.) pree-hi-**stawr**-ik
Describing something which happened before recorded (written) history.
Example
Stonehenge is the most famous prehistoric monument in Britain.

Post War (adj.) pohst wawr
Describes the period after a war, in Europe usually the **decade** after the end of WWII in 1945.
Example
In post war Europe a strong desire to prevent another war led to the formation of the EEC (a forerunner of the EU).

Ancient (adj.) **eyn**-sh*uh* nt
Describes something which occurred a very long time ago.
Example
The study of ancient history includes the civilizations of Greece and Rome which gave us the roots of thousands of English words.

Medieval (adj.) mee-dee-**ee**-v*uh* l
Describes something which occurred in the middle ages, roughly the 5 **centuries** between 1000 and 1500 AD, in European history.
Example
The most famous work of literature written in medieval England is Chaucer's Canterbury Tales.

Contemporary (adj.) k*uh* n-**tem**-p*uh*-rer-ee
Describes something that happens in the speaker's lifetime, so recent history.
Example
One of the major topics in contemporary history is the Cold War.

Power up your Vocabulary

Vocabulary in Use

In high school history classes, you will begin to study the sources of history; where the information comes from and how much **credibility** it has. On this page we will learn some vocabulary about historical sources.

Artifact (n) (c) **ahr**-t*uh*-fakt
An object or item of physical evidence of the past.
Example
Some of the most common **prehistoric** artifacts are pottery, jewellery and stone or metal tools.

Chronicle (n) (c) **kron**-i-k*uh* l
A book of history written in the dark ages (c500-1000AD) or middle ages and describing events in the writer's lifetime or **previously**.
Example
The Anglo-Saxon Chronicle is the main source for English history between the end of the Roman Empire and the beginning of the **medieval** period.

Manuscript (n) (c) **man**-y*uh*-skript
A document written by hand on paper or another material, not printed.
Example
A lot of **medieval** manuscripts have now been **digitized** to make them accessible to modern students.

Oral history (n) (I) **awr**-*uh* l **his**-t*uh*-ree
Historical information based on people's personal knowledge of past events.
Example
Oral history tells us about the experiences of ordinary people during major events such as World War II or the American civil rights movement.

Biased (adj.) **bahy**-*uh* st
A historical source is said to be biased when a writer or speaker gives only one side of an argument or story, deliberately or accidentally.
Example
Most advertising is biased because companies only want to tell the good things about their products.

Power up your Vocabulary

Section D, Unit 19, Lesson 2 - Geographical Vocabulary

Vocabulary in Use

In Unit 1 we looked at suffixes which tell you that a word is a noun e.g. **...tion, ...ment** etc. Suffixes can also tell you when a word is an adjective. We have already met **....able** in Unit 6. Can you remember what it means? In this lesson we will learn some adjectives to describe climate and add the suffixes:

                    .... **al** (adj.)   .... **ic** (adj.)

Arctic (adj.) **ahrk**-tik   **ahr**-tik
Describing something coming from the region of the North Pole; very cold.
Example
Northern Canada and Northern Russia both have arctic climates.

Arid (adj.) **ar**-id
Describing something which is very dry with very little rain.
Example
The Sahara Desert has one of the most arid climates in the world.

Equatorial (adj.) ee-kwuh-**tohr**-ee-uh l
Describing a climate which occurs close to the equator, hot and humid all year round.
Example
The Amazon basin of Brazil has an equatorial climate which gives rise to the rainforests.

Monsoon (adj.) mon-**soon**
Describing a climate where a lot of rain falls all in one season while the rest of the year is dry.
Example
Most of India has a monsoon climate.

Temperate (adj.) **tem**-per-it
Describing a climate which is neither extremely hot in summer nor extremely cold in winter.
Example
Britain and Northern Europe have temperate climates.

Power up your Vocabulary

Geographical Features

Archipelago (n) (c) ahr-k*uh*-**pel**-*uh*-goh
A large group of islands of varying sizes which often form a country.
Example
Indonesia has one of the world's largest archipelagos comprising more than 13,000 islands.

Canyon (n) (c) **kan**-y*uh* n
A very deep valley with steep sides usually with a river flowing along the bottom of the valley.
Example
The Grand Canyon in Colorado, USA is a famous tourist spot.

Fjord (n) (c) fyawrd   fyohrd
A long narrow bay or inlet with steep sides usually formed as a result of glacial erosion.
Examples
Norway is famous for the hundreds of fjords along its west coast which are a favorite destination for cruise ships.

Glacier (n) (c) **gley**-sher
A slow-moving river of ice flowing down a mountainside or into the sea.
Example
The many glaciers in the Antarctic are melting more quickly as a result of climate change which may raise sea levels in the future.

Plateau (n) (c) **plat**-oh
A large area of flat land situated at high altitude.
Example
The Tibetan Plateau in China is more than 4000 meters above sea level and is sometimes called "the roof of the world."

> ### Take it Further
>
> To find out more about the places, geographical features and climates mentioned in this lesson try:
>
> https://www.discovery.com/

Section D, Unit 19, Exercises

Exercise 1: Timeline

*Complete the timeline **chronologically** using words and phrases from the word bank. An example is given.*

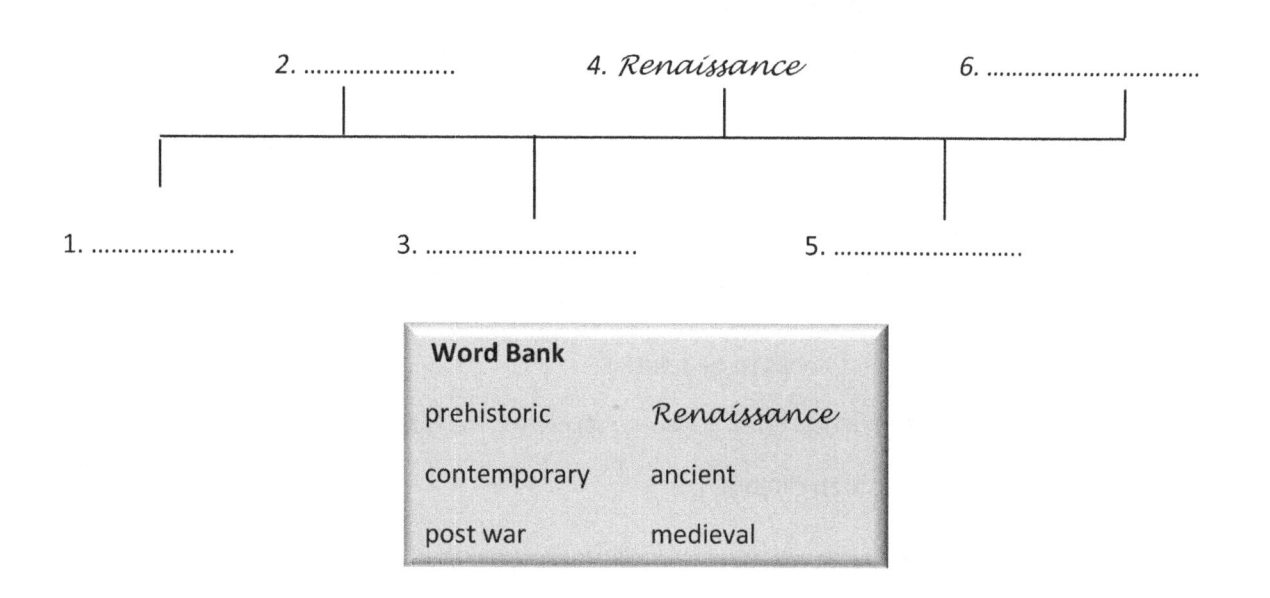

2. ……………….   4. *Renaissance*   6. ………………………

1. …………………   3. ……………………..   5. …………………….

Word Bank

prehistoric	*Renaissance*
contemporary	ancient
post war	medieval

Exercise 2: Labelling Pictures

Label the features below with words from this unit. The first one has been done for you.

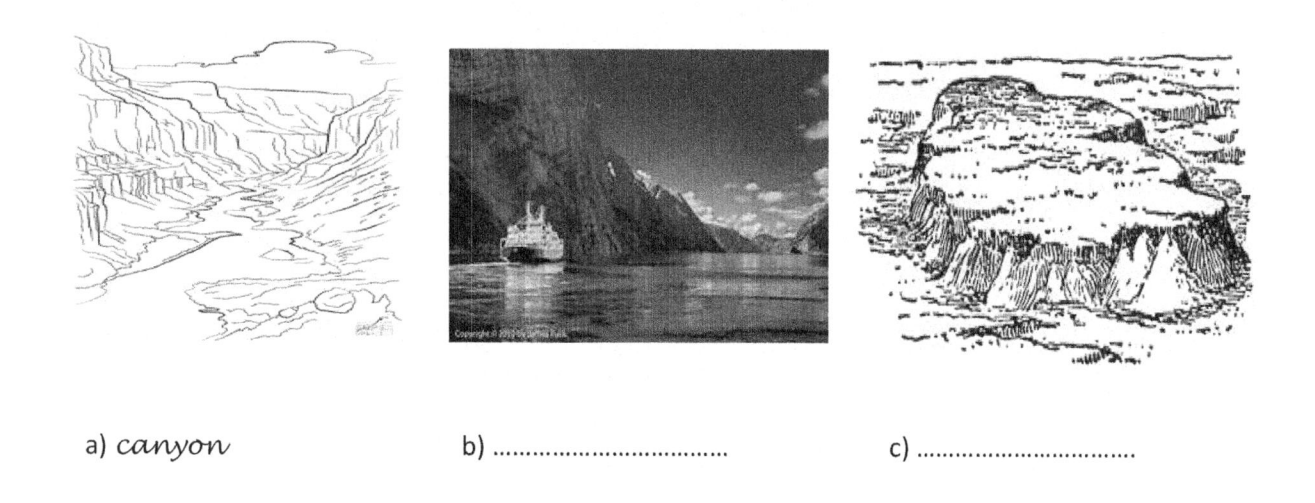

a) *canyon*   b) ………………………   c) ………………………

Power up your Vocabulary

d) ....

e) ....

Exercise 3: Correct the Mistakes

There is a misunderstanding in each of the following sentences. Rewrite the sentences so that they are factually correct. The first one has been done for you as an example

1. Manuscripts were among the first books to be printed.

    Manuscripts were not printed, they were written by hand.

2. The north of Canada has a monsoon climate.

    ....

3. The adjective **equatorial** describes something which occurs in the Arctic.

    ....

4. If a source is described as biased it means that it presents both sides of the argument about a historical event.

    ....

5. You can find information about **Euclid** and **Pythagoras** in a book of contemporary history.

    ....

6. The Sahara Desert is one of the least arid places on earth.

    ....

7. A book entitled "Post War Europe" is about the events before World War II started.

    ....

8. In a temperate climate people are always complaining that it is either too hot or too cold.

    ....

Section D, Unit 20, Lesson 1 - Economics Vocabulary

Vocabulary in Use

In Unit 19 we saw how prefixes can tell you part of the meaning of a word. In this unit we will meet two new prefixes:

Micro........ small (scale)
Macro....... large (scale)

Then we will go on to learn some basic words about economics. <u>Note:</u> Many of these words have other meanings in other contexts. See **Capital** (Unit 13 and this unit). The definitions given below are specific to economics.

Review

In Unit 10 we learned verbs for describing trends which go up and down. How many pairs of antonyms can you remember?

We also learned adverbs to describe trends more accurately. Which ones can you remember?

Microeconomics (n) (u) mahy-kroh-ek-*uh*-**nom**-iks

The branch of economics which is concerned with events on a small scale, often a single company.

<u>Example</u>
Every business owner needs to understand the laws of microeconomics relating to his/her enterprise.

Macroeconomics (n) (u) mak-roh-ek-*uh*-**nom**-iks

The branch of economics which is concerned with events on a large scale, usually a country or the entire world.

<u>Example</u>
Governments use macroeconomics to decide policies about trade, interest rates, employment and so on.

Demand (n) (I) dih-**mand**

(In economics) The total amount of a product or service which people wish to buy.

<u>Example</u>
In most cases, if the price of a product **falls** demand will **rise**.

Supply (n) (I) s*uh*-**plahy**

(In economics) The total amount of a product or service which is available to purchase.

<u>Example</u>
Under most circumstances if the supply of a product **increases** then the price will **decline**.

Power up your Vocabulary

Trade (n) (I) treyd
The practice of buying and selling goods or services either by barter or by using money.
Example
The total volume of trade between countries **has grown sharply** in the last few decades.

Import (v) (T), (n) (c) im-**pawrt**   Antonyms: **Export** (v) (T), (n) (c) ik-**spawrt**
The action of bringing goods and services into a country or sending goods and services to another country.
The goods and services brought into a country from elsewhere or sent to another country.
Example
Britain has to import tropical fruits such as bananas which do not grow in its **temperate** climate but exports a lot of cars.

Resources and Ownership

Capital (n) (u) **kap**-i-tl
Money or assets invested into a business.
Example
One of the most difficult aspects of starting a business is raising sufficient capital.

Labor (n) (u) **ley**-ber
Work carried out by the owner or employees of a business in order to produce goods or services.
Example
In the modern **knowledge economy** labor usually involves brainpower rather than muscle power.

Raw Material (n) (I) raw m*uh*-**teer**-ee-*uh* l
The substances which are processed in manufacturing to make a finished product.
Example
The main raw material used to make a T-shirt is cotton.

Nationalization (n) (u)   Antonym: **Privatization**
When the state takes over private businesses and they are run by the government.
Privatization is when the government sells nationalised industries to private shareholders.
Example
Nationalization was fashionable in **Post War** Europe but there has been a **trend** towards privatization programs in recent years.

Power up your Vocabulary

Section D, Unit 20, Lesson 2 - More Economics Vocabulary

> ## Vocabulary in Use
>
> In economics, you will study how well or badly a country or a business is performing. To do this, economists use a range of **yardsticks** to measure performance.
>
> **Yardstick** (n) (c) A measure or number used to judge performance.

Balance of payments (n) (u) **bal**-*uh* ns uv **pey**-m*uh* nts
The difference in value between the goods and services a country exports and those it imports.
Example
A country, such as Germany, which exports more than it imports has a balance of payments **surplus** (n) (c) **sur**-pl*uh*s.
A country which imports more than it exports, such as Britain, has a balance of payments **deficit** (n) (c) dih-**fis**-it

Gross Domestic Product (GDP) (n) (u) grohs d*uh*-**mes**-tik **prod**-*uh* kt
The total value of all the goods and services produced in a country, usually within one year.
Example
The United States has by far the largest GDP in the world but China is catching up fast.

Inflation (n) (u) in-**fley**-sh*uh* n   Antonym: **deflation** (n) (u) dih-**fley**-sh*uh* n
The rate at which prices are increasing or decreasing within a country, usually expressed as a percentage.
Example
Most economists think that an inflation rate of about 2% per year is healthy for the economy.

Unemployment rate (n) (u) uhn-em-**ploi**-m*uh* nt reyt   Antonym: **Full employment** (n) (u)
The number of people who do not have a job, usually expressed as a percentage of the total population of working age.
The situation when everyone who wants a job has one.
Example
Unemployment is always unpopular and most governments try to achieve full employment.

Power up your Vocabulary

Vocabulary in Use

On this page we will learn three new suffixes about people and ideas:
……… **ism** (n) (u) an idea or ideology associated with a person or movement
……. **ist** (adj.) (n) (c) someone who believes in the ideas of a thinker.
……. **ian** (adj.) (n) (c) someone who believes in the ideas of a thinker.

Note: ….ist and …ian are not interchangeable and there are no simple rules about which one to use with a particular person. Note examples.

Keynesian (adj.) (n) (u) **keyn**-zee-*uh* n
Describes the followers and ideas of a British economist of the 1930s and **post war** years.
Example: Keynesian economists believe that governments should intervene to help the economy during difficult times.

Marxism (n) (u) **Marxist** (adj.), (n) (c) **mahrk**-siz-*uh* m, **mahrk**-sist
The system of economic and political theories of the 19th century German economist and political philosopher, Karl Marx.
Describes the adherents of Karl Marx and his ideas.
Example: Marxist economists believe that the capitalist economic system cannot survive and will be overthrown.

Monetarism (n) (u) **Monetarist** (adj.), (n) (c) **muhn**-i-t*uh*-riz-*uh* m
The idea that the key to **macroeconomics** is to control the amount of money in the economy.
Describes the followers of Milton and Rose Friedman and their ideas.
Examples: Margaret Thatcher was strongly influenced by monetarist economics.

Word Families

Words with the root *economy* are one of the most commonly misused word families. Make sure you understand the differences between the following forms:
(The) **economy** (n) (I)   The overall economy of a country.
Economics (n) (u)   The academic study of economies.
Economist (n) (c)   An expert in economics.
Economic (adj.)   Describing something to do with economics.
Economic growth (n) u) The speed with which an economy is getting larger, usually measured by **GDP**.

Section D, Unit 20, Exercises

Exercise 1: Matching Definitions

Match the definitions with their keywords. Put the first letter of the correct keyword in the numbered spaces below to make the name of a famous economist. Who was he? The first one has been done for you.

1. (*g*) The study of the economics of a country or the world.   a) export
2. (   ) An economic theory which encourages government intervention in times of crisis.   b) nationalization
3. (   ) The action of sending goods or services to another country to sell.   c) Keynesian
4. (   ) A measure of the performance of an economy or economic policy.   d) economist
5. (   ) The policy of the state taking over private businesses usually associated with socialist or Marxist governments.   e) supply
6. (   ) An expert in economics who may teach in a university or work for a company.   f) yardstick
7. (   ) The total amount of good and services available for purchase in an economy.   *g) Macroeconomics*

John *M*aynard ....
           1   2   3   4   5   6   7

Exercise 2: Antonyms

Complete the table with the opposites of the words given. See the shaded example.

buy	*sell*	inflation	1.
unemployment	2.	3	deficit
4.	micro	nationalization	5.
6.	supply	7.	export

Power up your Vocabulary

Exercise 3: Describing Graphs

Use vocabulary from this unit as well as the verbs and adverbs from Unit 10 to describe the main trends in the following graphs showing changes in economic yardsticks. The first one has been started for you.

1. Figure 1: USA, Percentage GDP Growth 2014-18

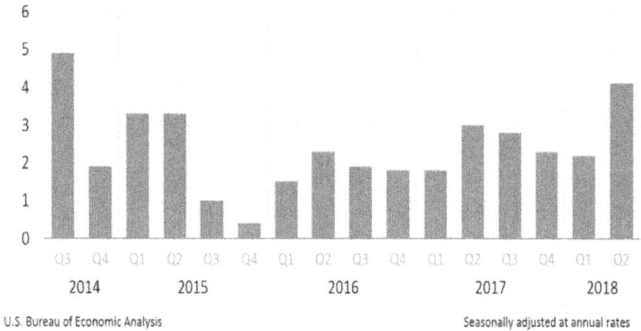

The graph shows that GDP growth in the USA fluctuated between 2014 and 2018.

....

....

2. Figure 2: India, Percentage Inflation Rate 2017-18

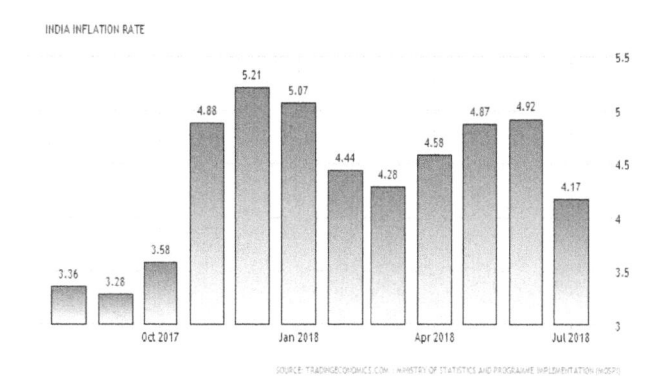

....

....

....

....

3. Figure 3: UK, Balance of Payments 1945-2017

....

....

....

....

Power up your Vocabulary

Section D, Unit 21, Lesson 1 - Arts Vocabulary

Vocabulary in Use

The arts may not be as important as maths or English but most schools provide a wide range of arts curriculum. Knowing arts vocabulary will enrich your overall vocabulary.

Review

In Unit 4 we learned strong adjectives for talking about movies and celebrities. They can also be used to describe other forms of the arts.

How many can you remember?

Types of the Arts

Performing arts (n) (plural) per-**fawrming** ahrts
A collective term for all kinds of live art done by performers including theatre, opera, ballet and circus.
<u>Examples</u>
Many large cities have a performing arts center such as the South Bank Complex in London.

Visual arts (n) (plural) **vizh**-oo-*uh* l ahrts
A collective term for arts which people look at or watch including cinema, painting and sculpture.
<u>Example</u>
The internet has increased the popularity of the visual arts by making images more accessible.

Opera (n) (l) **op**-r*uh*
A kind of performing art similar to a play except that the characters tell the story by singing.
<u>Example</u>
I went to the opera for the first-time last night. It was a school trip to see Handel's Messiah and the costumes and sets were just **mesmerizing**.

Ballet (n) (l) ba-**ley**
A kind of performing art in which the participants tell the story by dancing.
<u>Example</u>
Ballet is a national art form in Russia and Russian ballet companies are **renowned** all over the world.

Circus (n) (l) **sur**-k*uh* s
A kind of performing art which takes place in tents and features animals, clowns and acrobats.
<u>Example</u>
I went to the circus when I was on holiday. The clowns were **hilarious** but I thought the way they treated the performing elephants was **appalling**.

Power up your Vocabulary

Classical Music

Symphony (n) (c) **sim**-f*uh*-nee
A long and complex work of classical music typically written for an orchestra of many instruments.
Example
Beethoven (1770-1827) was among the most famous composers of symphonies.

Orchestra (n) (c) **awr**-k*uh*-str*uh*
A large group of musical instruments and their players typically organized in sections for strings, brass, woodwind and percussion instruments.
Example
I went to a concert by the Royal Philharmonic Orchestra recently and everyone looked so **well-groomed** and **well-heeled** that I felt out of place in jeans.

Conductor (n) (c) k*uh* n-**duhk**-ter
(in classical music) A person who instructs an orchestra how to play the music using a baton.
Example
Herbert von Karajan (1908-1989) became world famous as the conductor of the Berlin Philharmonic Orchestra.

Concerto (n) (c) k*uh* n-**cher**-toh
A work of classical music for one or more principle instruments with orchestral accompaniment.
Example
The 18th century Austrian composer Mozart (1756-1791) wrote 27 piano concertos most of which are still played regularly.

Score (n) (c) skohr
(in music) The papers on which music is written and which players follow when performing.
Example
The ability to read a musical score is an important stage in learning to play any instrument.

Section D, Unit 21, Lesson 2 - Visual Arts Vocabulary

> ## Review
>
> In Unit 20 we learned the suffixes **…..ism** and **….. ist** meaning an idea and its supporters. Can you remember any examples?
>
> In this lesson we will see how these suffixes are used in art. Notice how nouns ending in **...ism** are always uncountable but those ending in **….ist** and other person suffixes such as **…er** and **….or** are always countable.

Classical (adj.) **klas**-i-kuh l
Describes a period which is believed to set standards of excellence or norms to follow. In Art ancient Greece and Rome, in music the 18th and 19th centuries.
Example
A lot of classical art survives, especially in Italy, and has inspired later generations of artists.

Renaissance (adj.), (n) (u) ri-**ney**-s*uh* ns
The period from the 15th to 17th centuries which saw a great revival of creativity in the arts in Europe.
Example
Michelangelo (1475-1564) is one of the best-known artists of the Italian Renaissance.

Impressionism (n) (u) im-**presh**-*uh*-niz-*uh* m   Person: **Impressionist** (adj.), (n) (c) im-**presh**-*uh*-nist
A movement in 19th century art, principally in France, which reduced the level of detail in painting.
Example
The impressionists were laughed at by the art establishment of their time but are now very fashionable.

Cubism (n) (u) **kyoo**-biz-*uh* m   Person: **Cubist** (adj.), (n) (c) **kyoo**-biz-ist
A movement in 20th century art which reduced all objects to geometrical shapes.
Example:
Cubism is mainly associated with the Spanish painter Pablo Picasso (1881-1973).

Abstract (adj) ab-**strakt**
(in art) 20th century art which focused on form, line and color instead of depicting objects realistically.
Example: The abstract works of the American artist Jackson Pollock (1912-1966) now fetch very high prices at art auctions.

Power up your Vocabulary

Sculpture (n) (I) **skuhlp**-cher   Person: **Sculptor** (n) (c) skuhlp-ter
Three-dimensional art made from a solid block of material.

Carve (v) (T) kahrv
(in art) The action of making a work of art by cutting and polishing a material, typically stone, wood or ivory.
<u>Example</u>
A lot of African art is carved from wood or ivory with great skill.

Cast (v) (T) kast
(in art) The process of making a work of art by pouring hot, liquid metal into a mould to make a shape.
<u>Example</u>
The **ancient** Chinese knew how to cast bronze to make **amazing** art objects such as the chariots found with the terracotta warriors guarding the tomb of the Emperor Qin Shi Shuang Di at Xian.

Bust (n) (c) buhst
(in art) A portrait of the head and shoulders of a person, male or female, usually carved in stone or cast in bronze.
<u>Example</u>
A bronze bust of King David by Michelangelo is one of the most **iconic** pieces of **Renaissance** art.

Plinth (n) (c) plinth
(in art) The base on which a sculpture stands.
<u>Example</u>
The Statue of Liberty stands on a stone plinth in New York harbor which makes it visible for miles.

Marble (n) (u) **mahr**-b*uh* l
A type of stone which occurs naturally in a variety of beautiful colors and is popular with sculptors.
<u>Example</u>
Marble was widely used in **classical** and **Renaissance** art because it was easy to work and **durable**.

Durable (adj.) **doo** r-*uh*-b*uh* l
Describes something which has the quality of lasting for a long time.

> ### Take it Further
>
> To find out more about the artists and musicians mentioned in this lesson search: https://www.biography.com/. Don't forget to make notes of new words you find.

Section D, Unit 21, Exercises

Exercise 1: Sentence Completion
Complete each sentence with a word of phrase from the word bank.

Example

Marble is a material which occurs naturally in beautiful colors and is often used by sculptors.

Word Bank

marble   circus   bust   Conductor

cubism   impressionist

concerto   abstract   carves

1. Modern art which focuses on form, color and line and does not try to depict an object realistically is called .... Art.

2. The person who directs an orchestra is called a ....

3. British stamps and coins often show a sculpture of the head and shoulders of the queen known as a ....

4. Claude Monet is perhaps the best-known artist of the .... school.

5. You can expect to find clowns and acrobats performing in a ....

6. A sculptor .... his art from a block of wood or stone.

7. The concept of reducing objects to geometrical forms in art is called ....

8. A piano .... features a pianist accompanied by an orchestra.

Exercise 2: Anagrams
Unscramble the letters to make words from this unit. The first one has been done for you.

1. ltebal   *ballet*   2. crtbasta   ....

3. pysyhnom   ....   4. crisaensane ....

5. ulasiv tasr ....   6. tcsa   ....

7. lemrba   ....   8. htrcoaesr   ....

Exercise 3: Crossword

Across
3. A 19th century French art movement.
5. Art made by carving something out of wood or stone.
7. To make art by pouring liquid metal into a mould.

Down
1. Arts of this type are live and include the theatre.
2. Music written on paper for players to follow.
4. An art form in which a story is told by singing.
6. Describing the music composed by Beethoven and Mozart.

Power up your Vocabulary

Section D, Unit 22, Lesson 1 - Literary Vocabulary

Genre (n) (c) **zhahn**-r*uh*
A style or category of art, usually a type of literature e.g. a novel.
Example: Most writers stick to the same genre throughout their careers.

Allegory (n) (c) **al**-*uh*-gawr-ee
A genre of short story intended to teach a moral lesson.
Example: The story of the boy who cried wolf is a classic allegory.

Memoirs (n) (usually plural) **mem**-wahrz
A type of non-fiction book usually written by a celebrity or politician at the end of their career.
Example: Memoirs are often written to **justify** the author's actions, so they are sometimes **biased.**

Narrative (n) (I) **nar**-*uh*-tiv
A genre of writing, either fiction or non-fiction, which tells a story, usually in **chronological** order.
Example: John Steinbeck's novel "Grapes of Wrath" is a powerful narrative which tells the story of the Joad family's struggles during the American Depression in the 1930s.

Satire (n) (I) **sat**-ahy*uh* r
A genre of writing which seeks to make something seem morally wrong or **absurd** by using humor, sarcasm or ridicule.
Example: Gulliver's Travels by Jonathan Swift, which is now read as a children's book, was originally a satire on 18th century British politics.

Study Tip

Word families crop up again with literary vocabulary.
Examples:
Narrate (v) (T)   Narrative (n) (c)   Narrator (n) (c) person
Satirize (v) (T)   Satire (n) (I)   Satirist (n) (c) person   Satirical (adj.)   Satirically (adv)

Always ask yourself what you want a word to do in a sentence e.g. name something, describe an action or modify a noun or a verb. This will help you choose the correct form.

Vocabulary in Use

To succeed in high school and college you will have to learn skills for both academic and creative writing. There are now some great online writing laboratories (OWLs) to help you. But most of them use technical terms to talk about **literary devices** used in writing.

Literary device (n) (c) A technique used by writers to achieve a particular effect.

In this unit we will learn some creative writing terms to help you make the most of the resources available.

Hook (n) (c) h*oo*k
(In writing) An introduction which attracts the reader's attention and makes them want to read more.
Example: A good hook can be an interesting fact or figure or an anecdote.

Anecdote (n) (c) **an**-ik-doht
A short, interesting or amusing account of an incident or event; usually personal and often used as a hook to attract reader's attention.
Example: "The Crucible" by Arthur Miller begins with a good example of an anecdote.

Theme (n) (c) theem
(In writing) The main, unifying idea of a novel, short story or play.
Example: The theme of Charlotte Bronte's classic novel "Jane Eyre" is that love can overcome class barriers and moral conventions.

Setting (n) (c) **set**-ing
The context in which something occurs; in a novel or short story the place and time in which the action takes place.
Example: In "The Loneliness of the Long-Distance Runner" by Alan Sillitoe the setting is a prison for young boys in 1950s England.

Climax (n) (c) **klahy**-maks
The point in a story or speech when all the threads of the plot come together in a dramatic ending.
Example: The famous "I have a dream …" quotation was the climax of a speech by Martin Luther King.

Section D, Unit 22, Lesson 2 – Drama and Poetry Vocabulary

Drama

Dramatist (n) (c) **dram**-*uh*-tist
A person who writes plays.
Example
Henrik Ibsen (1828-1906) was a great Norwegian dramatist whose works have been translated into many languages.

Antagonist (n) (c) an-**tag**-*uh*-nist
(In writing) One or more characters involved in a conflict situation which may be the theme of a novel, short story or play.
Example
In Romeo and Juliet by William Shakespeare the antagonists are the feuding families, the Montagues and the Capulets.

Cast (n) (c) kast
(In literature cf. Unit 21) A collective noun for all the actors and actresses who appear in a play or movie.
Example
The musicals written by the dramatist Andrew Lloyd Webber usually have an all-star cast when performed in London's West End theatres.

Soliloquy (n) (c) s*uh*-**lil**-*uh*-kwee
A speech in a play in which a character appears to be talking to him/herself.
Example
Soliloquies are a literary device often used by dramatists to communicate a change in the setting or a stage in the plot to the audience.

Denouement (n) (c) dé·noue·ment
A synonym for climax often used to describe the ending of a complicated plot in a play or novel.
Example
Arthur Miller (1915-2005) wrote a classic example of a tragic denouement in "Death of a Salesman".

Power up your Vocabulary

Poetry

Meter (n) (I) **mee**-ter
(In poetry) The rhythmic structure of a verse, or set of lines in a poem often involving long and short syllables.
Example
Shakespeare used a special type of meter called iambic pentameter (5 short and 5 long syllables alternately).

Rhyme (v) (T), (n) (I) rahym
Two or more words where the last syllable of each word has the same sound usually used as the last word of a line in poetry.
Example
The words bound, found, round and sound all end with the same sound, so they rhyme.

Saga (n) (c) **sah**-g*uh*
A long poem written as **oral history** to remember heroic actions or adventures and pass on the story to the next generation.
Example
Sagas are particularly associated with the Viking cultures of Norway and Iceland.

Elegy (n) (c) **el**-i-jee
A sad poem written in memory of a dead person.
Example
Thomas Grey (1716-1771) wrote "Elegy Written in a Country Churchyard" which is still one of the most celebrated poems in the English language.

Couplet (n) (c) **kuhp**-lit
Two consecutive lines of poetry/verse which rhyme.
Example
Romantic couplets written in letters or greeting cards were popular for centuries before being replaced by e mails and texting.

> ### Take it Further
>
> To find out more about the writers, poets and dramatists mentioned in this unit search:
>
> https://www.biography.com/

Section D, Unit 22, Exercises

Exercise 1: Word Search

Find the words in the puzzle. Words may be horizontal, vertical or diagonal. Spellings may be forwards or backwards. One example has been highlighted for you.

Literary Word Search

```
C R H R I S T O P T H E R M A
R E L O W E K J S J D H E P Q
E T O U H T P I U K O Y P Y O
K E M R K D T G B M I L U C T
W M R A B A Y C D N J Q R E L
X M U I M A N T A G O N I S T
E V H A T V J O S L W R O J K
R L R W S A U T I N O A Y F Q
K D E X C J S L S R I O M E M
N C J G O L O H B S Z D L Z I
U T U X Y S I G B U C Z G M J
D B F Y M I C M E S I Q U Z V
A N E C D O T E A N N K Q J M
V N M U Z C Z A Q X R H B E L
Q C W X T M Z C V N H E E S W
```

ANECDOTE   ANTAGONIST   CLIMAX
DRAMATIST   ELEGY   GENRE
MEMOIRS   METER   SATIRE
SOLILOQUY

Power up your Vocabulary

Exercise 2: Multiple Choice

Choose the best answer for each of the following questions. The first one has been done for you.

1. (*c*) Which of the following is a long poem written to commemorate the heroic actions of a leader:

    a) an elegy   b) a couplet   *c) a saga*   d) a ballad

2. (   ) Which of the following is the best definition of a hook in literature:

    a) An introduction which states the theme of the story
    b) A conclusion which brings the threads of the plot together
    c) A conflict between two or more characters in the story.
    d) An introduction which captures the reader's attention.

3. (   ) Which of the following literary devices involves a character apparently talking to him/herself:

    a) anecdote   b) soliloquy   c) hook   d) couplet

4. (   ) The actors and actresses in a play are collectively known as:

    a) The cast   b) The choir   c) The audience   d) The dramatists

5. (   ) Which <u>two</u> of the following terms describe the ending of a complex plot in a
   (   ) novel or play:

    a) denouement   b) storyline   c) climax   d) meter

6. (   ) Satire can be described as:

    a) The use of facts to justify an opinion.   b) A way of remembering heroic deeds.

    c) The story of a famous person's life.

    d) The use of humor or ridicule to make something or someone appear absurd.

7. (   ) Celebrities sometimes write their memoirs in order to:

    a) Explain and justify their actions
    b) Make themselves more famous.
    c) Announce their plans for the future.
    d) Antagonize their enemies.

8. (   ) The theme of a novel or play is:

    a) It's title   b) It's main character   c) It's main idea   d) It's genre

Power up your Vocabulary

Exercise 3: Complete a Vocabulary Usage Table
Complete the missing words in the following table. The first one has been done for you.

Word	Phonic spelling	Part of speech	Usage e.g. countable/uncountable	Synonym
(1) e*legy*	**el**-i-jee	noun	countable	xxxxxxxxx
dramatist	**dram**-*uh*-tist	(2) _____	countable	playwright
climax	(3) _____	noun	countable	(4) _____
setting	**set**-ing	noun	(5) _____	xxxxxxxxx
(6) _____	rahym	verb, noun	transitive, countable or uncountable	xxxxxxxxx
contemporary	k*uh* n-**tem**-p*uh*-rer-ee	(7) _____ + noun	countable	xxxxxxxxx
(8) _____	theem	noun	countable	main idea

Power up your Vocabulary

Section D, Unit 23, Lesson 1 - Media Vocabulary

Tabloid (newspaper) (n) (c) **tab**-loid
A type of newspaper printed on small pages and specializing in stories about crime, scandal, celebrities and sport.
Example
Tabloid newspapers are often critized for simplifying or distorting news and intruding into people's private lives.

Exclusive adj, (n) (c) ik-**skloo**-siv
(In the media) Describing a story which only one newspaper knows about.
Example
Tabloid newspapers compete for exclusive stories, for example, about the love lives of celebrities.

Broadsheet (newspaper) (n) (c) **brawd**-sheet
A type of newspaper printed on larger pages than a tabloid and covering more serious news topics in greater depth.
Example
Some broadsheet newspapers can have a considerable influence on current affairs.

Correspondent (n) (u) kawr-*uh*-**spon**-d*uh*nt
A newspaper or TV reporter who specializes in a particular topic.
Example
Kate Adie became well known as the war correspondent of the CNN reporting on the conflicts in Iraq and Afghanistan.

Byline (n) (c) **bahy**-lahyn
The name of the journalist who researched and wrote a newspaper article, usually just below the headline.
Example
A story with a byline has more **credibility** as a source for **assignments** or **presentations.**

Power up your Vocabulary

Review

In Unit 8 we learned reporting verbs. The more common ones are widely use in media reports. Can you remember the meaning of **announce, assume, assert, disclose, deny, infer, imply, reject**?

In this lesson we will add more similar verbs used in the media. Remember most of them have word families. Make sure you are using the correct word form.

Investigate (v) in-**ves**-ti-geyt   (noun) **investigation**   (adj.) **investigative**
The action of newspapers or TV programs doing research to find a story, often about the effects of public policy.
Example
It can be argued that the media must have the right to carry out investigative journalism.

Publish (v) (I) **puhb**-lish   (noun) **publication**
The action of printing a newspaper, magazine or book or posting online information or opinions.
Example
Online news is becoming more and more popular because it is more up to date than traditional newspapers which only publish once a day.

Allege (v) (T) *uh*-**lej**   (noun) **allegation**
To state without evidence that something, usually involving crime or incompetence, is true.
Example
Newspapers sometimes allege that a celebrity is involved in crime or is having an affair.

Incite (v) (T) in-**sahyt**
To encourage someone to behave in a certain way, often by using strong language.
Example
Social media are often **accused** of inciting hatred and intolerance in society.

Retract (v) (T) ri-**trakt**   (noun) **retraction**
The action of withdrawing an allegation, accusation or published research that has been shown to be false.
Example
A growing number of medical and scientific papers have been retracted in recent years.

Power up your Vocabulary

Section D, Unit 23, Lesson 2 - Crime and Law Vocabulary

Vocabulary in Use

Perhaps the most common topic in the media is crime and the law. This topic has its own specialist vocabulary. We will start with some common verbs.

Legislate (v) (I) **lej**-is-leyt
The action of passing a law to control something e.g. by a congress.
Example
The media often campaign for Parliament to legislate to ban something they regard as harmful e.g. advertising on children's TV.

Enforce (v) (T) en-**fawrs**
The action of catching and punishing those who break a law.
Example
It is the responsibility of the police and the courts to enforce the law.

Commit (a crime) (v) (T) k*uh*-**mit**
(in law) The action of doing something that the law has defined as a crime.
Example
The Victorian serial killer known as Jack the Ripper committed at least five murders.

Remand (v) (T) ri-**mand**
To return a criminal to police custody or prison after an appearance in court.
Example
People who have been arrested are often remanded in custody while the case against them is prepared for trial.

Sentence (n) (I), (v) (T) **sen**-tns
(verb in law) To announce the punishment to be given to a criminal when he has been found guilty of an offense.
Example
It is the responsibility of the judge to sentence a criminal after taking account of all the evidence in the case against him/her.

Power up your Vocabulary

Vocabulary in Use

We have seen in previous units how adjectives can collocate with nouns and adverbs can collocate with verbs to make common expressions. On this page we will look at some more examples related to crime and the law. Some of these are pairs of opposites (antonyms).

Lenient (adj.) **lee**-nee- uh nt
(of a sentence) Describes a lesser punishment than the maximum allowed by law or expected by public opinion or the media.
Example
Many people believe that sentences for crimes against women are too lenient in some countries.

Draconian (adj.) druh-**koh**-nee-uh n
(of a sentence) Describes the maximum possible sentence or a sentence which public opinion or the media consider to be too harsh.
Example
The sentences given to the Great Train Robbers were widely considered to be draconian.

Extenuating (adj.) ik-**sten**-yoo-ey-ting
(of circumstances) Describes factors which make a crime less serious and usually reduces the sentence passed by the judge.
Example
Self-defence is regarded as an extenuating circumstance in some cases of violent crime.

Aggravating (adj.) **ag**-ruh-vey-ting
(of circumstances) Describes factors which make a crime more serious and increase the sentence passed by the judge.
Example
Using a knife or a gun while committing a robbery is an aggravating circumstance.

Rigorously (adv.) **rig**-er-uhs-lee
To do something strongly and consistently with no exceptions.
Example
Laws against drink driving have been rigorously enforced in recent years.

Section D, Lesson 23, Exercises

Exercise 1: Cloze Test
Complete the following passage from a newspaper crime report using words from this unit. The first letter is given to help you.

17 Years for armed robber who terrorized the town

Agnes Palliser, crime (1) **c**......................

At Anytown Crown Court today Leroy Smith was found guilty of six charges of armed robbery. He was (2) **s**.................. to 17 years in jail by the judge Mr Justice Robertson. Smith, 23 of Anderson Court in the town, had **denied** the charges. Earlier David Mason Lawyer summed up the prosecution case by **accusing** Smith of deliberately targeting vulnerable, elderly people as his victims. Mason added that Smith had (3) **c**...................... six crimes over an eight- month period last year. Smith picked the location of his attacks to avoid CCTV cameras Mason said. Smith also wore a mask to hide his identity and **terrify** his victims. It took a six-month (4) **i**............................ by the police to identify and catch Smith who had terrorized the town. The judge praised their efforts to rigorously (5) **e**......................... the law and protect the public. In Smith's defence his barrister, Tony Andrews Lawyer claimed that Smith had limited intelligence, was easily led and had been (6) **i**...................... by others to act as he did. Passing sentence, the judge described Smith's offenses as "**appalling** acts." He added that Smith had a "**dreadful**" previous criminal record and that his lawyer had failed to prove that others were involved. Furthermore, the offenses were planned and the use of a mask and a knife were (7) **a**.......................... circumstances which left him no alternative but to impose a severe sentence. But speaking outside the court afterwards, Smith's family admitted that he had been carrying a knife but pointed out that he had not used it, none of his victims had been seriously injured and the amounts stolen were trivial. They called the sentence (8) **d**............................ and said that Smith would appeal.

Power up your Vocabulary

Exercise 2: Matching Definitions

Match a keyword in Group A with a definition in Group B. The first one has been done for you.

Group A

1. (A) broadsheet   2. (   ) retract

3. (   ) remand   4. (   ) exclusive

5. (   ) lenient   6. (   ) publish

7. (   ) legislate   8. (   ) extenuating

Group B

(n) The action of making laws to allow or ban something.

(l) To withdraw allegations or information that has been proved false.

(a) An adjective which describes a story published by only one newspaper.

(C) To send a criminal back to jail after an appearance in court.

(p) A sentence in criminal law which is less than the maximum allowed or less than the public thinks is justified.

(e) Circumstances which reduce the seriousness of a crime and the sentence imposed for it.

(A) *This type of large size newspaper investigates serious news topics in depth.*

(o) The action of printing in a newspaper, magazine or book, or posting online, information or opinions.

Now put the letters of the definitions in numerical order to make the name of one of the most **notorious** American criminals of all time.

           A ....
           1   2   3   4   5   6   7   8

Power up your Vocabulary

Exercise 3: Matching Suffixes

Complete the diagram with words from this unit ending with the suffixes shown. The first one has been done for you.

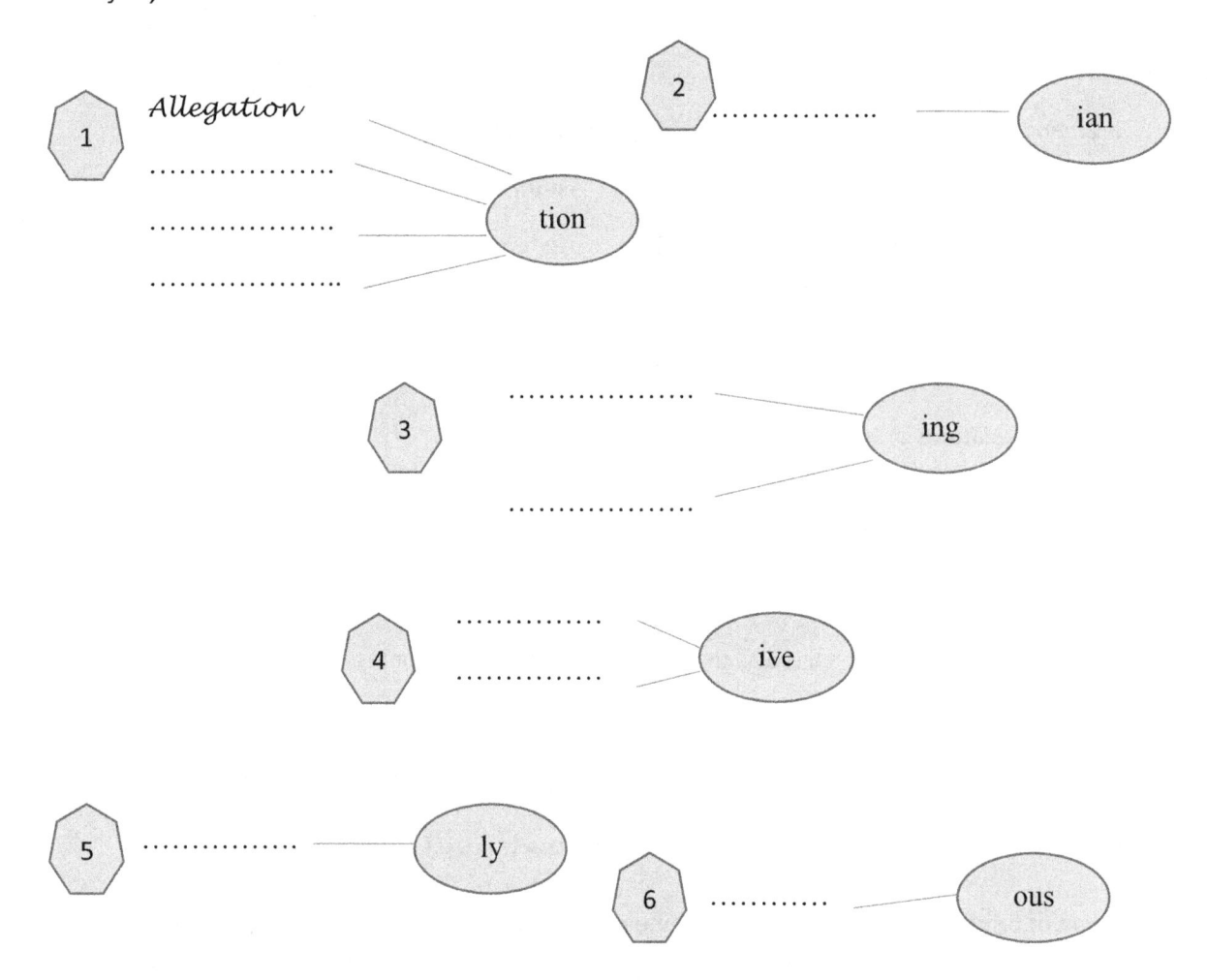

1. *Allegation*
   ....
   ....
   .... → tion

2. .... → ian

3. ....
   .... → ing

4. ....
   .... → ive

5. .... → ly

6. .... → ous

Now place the numbered groups of suffixes in the table of parts of speech

Nouns	Adjectives	Adverbs
1		

Power up your Vocabulary

Section D, Unit 24, Lesson 1 - Citizenship Vocabulary

Vocabulary in Use

Good schools teach you to pass exams, of course. But they also teach you to become a responsible citizen. This means lessons concerning society, relationships, health and religion. In this unit we will learn vocabulary for some of the concepts involved.

Review

In Unit 1 and Unit 20 we learned some noun suffixes. Which ones can you remember? Give examples. Vocabulary for behavior and personality also uses other suffixes. In this unit we will add:

…….ence   ….. ness

Inclusiveness (n) (u) in-**kloo**-siv-nes
The practice of treating everyone as an equal regardless of gender, ethnicity, disability etc. and encouraging them to take part in school, work and social activities.
Example: Inclusiveness is seen as increasingly important to make maximum use of human abilities.

Multiculturalism (n) (u) mul-tee-**kuhl-**cher-uh-liz-uh m
The idea that people can maintain different cultures while living in the same society based on mutual respect.
Example: The concept of multiculturalism is very controversial in many countries.

Tolerance (n) (u) **tol**-er-*uh* ns
Willingness to accept the right of others to have different opinions, and behave differently, from yourself.
Example: Tolerance is essential to live peacefully in a society with people from many countries.

Diversity (n) (u) dih-**vur**-si-tee
The state of being different in many ways.
Example: Some companies now believe diversity among their workforce is an advantage because it gives management access to a wider range of opinions.

Empathy (n) (u) **em**-p*uh*-thee
The ability to listen to and understand the point of view of others.
Example: People who have empathy always have lots of friends because they are good listeners.

Health

Nutrition (n) (u) noo-**trish**-*uh* n
The process of the human body converting food to energy; the study of healthy eating in humans.
Example
Good nutrition is about having a balanced diet and eating in moderation.

Obesity (n) (u) oh-**bee**-si-tee
The condition of being so overweight that it is dangerous for your health.
Example
Doctors are very worried about the growing number of children who are suffering from obesity.

Epidemic (adj), (n) (c) ep-i-**dem**-ik
A situation where large numbers of people in a community have the same disease at the same time.
Example
Obesity in Western countries is an example of an epidemic.

Addiction (n) (I) *uh*-**dik**-sh*uh* n
The condition of being physically and mentally dependent on a substance or activity.
Example
Addiction to computer games is a problem among teenagers in many countries.

Fitness (n) (u) **fit**-nis
The state of using exercise and good nutrition to become healthier.
Example
Most schools require students to take health education and PE classes in order to improve their fitness.

Power up your Vocabulary

Section D, Unit 24, Lesson 2 - Ethics and Beliefs

Ethics (n) (u) *eth*-iks
A system of moral principles used to decide whether actions are right or wrong.
<u>Example</u>
Ethics are the basis of most discussions about what is the right thing to do in any situation.

Compassion (n) (u) k*uh* m-*pash*-*uh* n
The quality of caring about those who have suffered misfortune, or are less well off than yourself.
<u>Example</u>
Most religions and systems of ethics teach that compassion is a duty.

Awareness (n) (u) *uh*-**wair**-nis
The state of having knowledge or understanding of something.
<u>Example</u>
Citizenship classes try to raise your awareness of the ethics and risks of smoking, getting drunk or taking drugs.

Avoidance (n) (l) *uh*-**void**-ns
The state of choosing to take actions in order to avert risk or danger.
<u>Example</u>
It is important to learn strategies for the avoidance of danger in personal relationships either online or face to face.

Consent (n) (l) k*uh* n-**sent**
Agreement to do something, or allow something to be done to you, usually with awareness of the consequences.
<u>Example</u>
It is a basic principle in ethics and law that in relationships all parties should consent to what is happening.

Study Tip

The noun suffixes ….. ance ……ence …..ness usually refer to states or conditions. They are nearly always uncountable. Remember this will affect the agreements with verbs, pronouns, demonstratives etc. when you use these words in sentences.

Faith (n) (I) feyth
Belief in something which cannot be touched or seen and which cannot be proved, or disproved by scientific evidence.
<u>Example</u>
The most common examples of faith are belief in a God or Gods.

Religion (n) (c) ri-**lij**-*uh* n
A set of beliefs and practices associated with faith in the existence of, and teachings of, one or more Gods.
<u>Example</u>
Religions have profoundly affected the culture and history of most countries.

Spirituality (n) (u) spir-i-choo-**al**-i-tee
The belief that human beings are more than biology and have a spirit or soul.
<u>Example</u>
Some people think that the materialism and selfishness of modern society is causing people to turn back to spirituality in search of a deeper meaning in life.

Theology (n) (u) thee-**ol**-*uh*-jee
The academic study of Gods and religions.
<u>Example</u>
In **medieval** Europe most universities were founded for the study of theology.

Worship (n) (c) **wur**-ship
The practice of acknowledging the power of God by praying, singing, reading holy books or meditating.
<u>Example</u>
Most religions set aside specific buildings such as churches, temples or mosques as places of worship.

Power up your Vocabulary

Section D, Unit 24, Exercises

Exercise 1: Correct the Mistakes

There is one mistake in each of the following sentences. It may be the meaning or form of a word. Find and correct it.

Example
Faith is belief in something based on scientific evidence.
Faith is belief in something even though it cannot be proved by scientific evidence.

1. Multiculturalness is about a society in which people of different cultures live together based on tolerance and respect.

   ....

2. Theology is the study of ethics and takes place in universities.

   ....

3. Nouns formed with the suffix ….ness are usually uncountable and refer to a person.

   ....

4. America is suffering from an epidemic of childhood obesement.

   ....

5. Students need to learn strategies for the voidence of risk when using websites for research.

   ....

6. Teachers should show awarenesses of diversity when preparing lesson plans in schools in **cosmopolitan** cities.

   ....

Exercise 2: Independent Writing

Choose any six of the concepts in this unit and write your own sentences giving an example of the meaning.

Power up your Vocabulary

Exercise 3: Word Puzzle

Match the definitions in the table below with words in this unit. Then fill in the squares, one letter in each square in the puzzle below. The first one has been done for you. The shaded squares will then form the name of a philosopher whose ideas still play a key role in modern concepts of ethics and citizenship. Who was he?

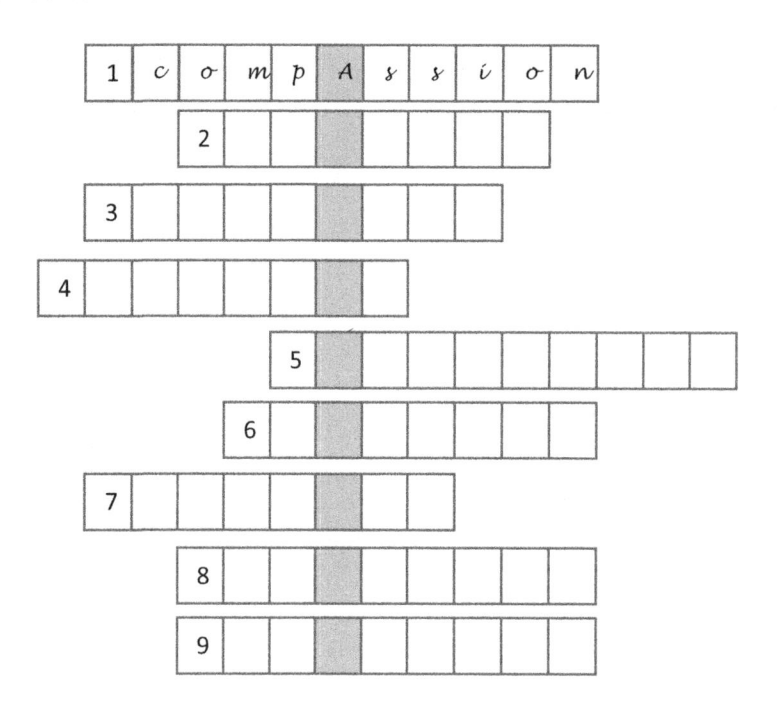

| 1 | c | o | m | p | A | s | s | i | o | n |

1. *A duty to care for the less fortunate.*
2. Showing respect to god e.g. by praying or singing.
3. The study of healthy eating.
4. Being healthy as a result of good nutrition and plenty of exercise.
5. Allowing others to have different opinions or behaviors from yourself.
6. Agreement to do something or have something done to you e.g. start a relationship.
7. Understanding someone else's point of view often by listening.
8. The practice of worshiping a God and following their teachings in your daily life.
9. The study of Gods and religions.

Take it Further

To find out more about the philosopher you have identified see:
https://kids.kiddle.co/Aristotle

Section D, Unit 25, Lesson 1 - Sports Vocabulary

> ## Vocabulary in Use
>
> We have looked a lot at suffixes on this book because they are so important for learning how to work out the meaning of words you may not know. We have learned some common suffixes for nouns, adjectives and adverbs. There are also some suffixes which tell you that a word is a verb e.g. …… **ate**
>
> Let's look at some examples in the field of sport. Notice that the noun forms do not always have the same suffixes even though the verbs do.

Commentate (v) (T)   **kom**-*uh* n-teyt   Noun: **Commentator** (c) **kom**-*uh* n-tey-ter
The action of describing an event e.g. sport to an audience either live or in a **broadcast.**
Example: Sports stars sometimes commentate after they have retired from competing, for example the cricketer Geoffrey Boycott.

Participate (v) (T) pahr-**tis**-*uh*-peyt   Noun: **Participant** (c) pahr-**tis**-*uh*-p*uh* nt
The action of taking part in a sport either to win or just for fun and exercise.
Example: The London Olympic Games organizers promised to increase the number of people who regularly participate in sport.

Pontificate (v) (T) pon-**tif**-i-keyt
The action of giving an opinion about something, usually formally and speaking as an expert.
Example: Some people think that former footballers who have become TV presenters pontificate too much about the game.

Officiate (v) (T) *uh*-**fish**-ee-eyt   Noun: **Official** (c) *uh*-**fish**-*uh* l
The action of interpreting and **enforcing** the rules in a sport.
Example: The highest honour for any football referee is to officiate at the World Cup finals.

Spectate (v) (T) **spek**-teyt   Noun: **Spectator** (c) **spek**-tey-ter
The action of watching a live event e.g. sports match, without participating in it.
Example: Far more people spectate at sports such as horse racing or motor racing than participate because of the cost and danger.

Power up your Vocabulary

> **Study Tip**
>
> A lot of sports vocabulary is specific to one sport. Compounds and collocations are important. It also helps to use the methods of classification we have studied on this book such as spidergrams, tables and trees to learn sports vocabulary. We will look at three categories in this unit; people, places and equipment.

People

Athlete (n) (c) **ath**-leet
Specifically, a participant in track and field (e.g. running, jumping etc) but can be used for other sports as well.
Example
Participants in the Olympic Games live in an athlete's village.

Clerk of the course (n) (c) klahrk ov the kohrs
The official in charge of an event in motor racing and horse racing.
Example
In motor racing the clerk of the course has to decide whether a competitor has driven dangerously.

Judge (n) (c) juhj
(in sport) An official who awards points based on how well a competitor has performed compared to a set of standards.
Example
Judges award scores and decide the winners in sports such as boxing, diving and gymnastics.

Referee (n) (c) ref-uh-**ree**
The most common term for the official who decides on what is fair or unfair in a sporting competition e.g. football, rugby, football and basketball.
Example
Referees nearly always wear a uniform and use a whistle to control the game.

Umpire (n) (c) **uhm**-pahyuhr
Another term for the official who decides what is fair or unfair and enforces the rules of a sport.
Example
The term umpire is usually used in sports which date from the 18th century or earlier and were originally played by the upper classes e.g. cricket and tennis.

Power up your Vocabulary

Section D, Unit 25, Lesson 2 - Places and Equipment in Sport

> ## Vocabulary in Use
>
> Some places to play sport are obvious such as court, ground and pitch. But how many compounds and collocations can you think of?
>
> <u>Examples</u>
> Cricket pitch   Football ground   Tennis court

Places

Course (n) (c) kohrs
A series of obstacles which competitors in a sport have to negotiate one or more times.
<u>Example:</u> A golf course usually has 18 holes and a series of obstacles such as trees, bunkers and lakes to make it challenging for the players.

Marina (n) (c) m*uh*-**ree**-n*uh*
A venue for water sports such as **yachting** which usually includes a harbor and a clubhouse.
<u>Example:</u> Cowes, on the Isle of Wight, has a well-known marina which is used for yachting and powerboat racing.

Stadium (n) (c) **stey**-dee-*uh* m
A large venue, usually circular or oval in shape, with seating for a large crowd of **spectators**.
<u>Example:</u> The Bird's Nest Stadium in Beijing, built for the 2008 Olympic Games, has become an **iconic** feature of the city.

Track (n) (c) trak
A type of course usually with an artificial surface which competitors have to go around, often many times, during a competition.
<u>Example:</u> An international athletics track is normally 400 meters long and during 10,000 meters race athletes have to complete 25 laps of the track.

Velodrome (n) (c) **vee**-l*uh*-drohm
A type of sports venue with a banked circular track and seating for spectators.
<u>Example:</u> Velodromes are specific to competitive cycling.

Power up your Vocabulary

Equipment

Golf club (n) (c) golf kluhb
A thin tube about 3 feet long made of steel or carbon fiber with a handle at the top and an oval shaped foot which is swung in an arc to hit a golf ball.

Squash racket (n) (c) skwosh **rak**-it
This object has an oval shaped head with a frame made of wood or carbon fiber and crisscrossed with taut strings. The head is joined to a handle about 30 centimeters long also made of wood or carbon fiber. It is held in one hand and used to hit a ball around a squash court.

Saber (n) (c) **sey**-ber
A slender object about 2 feet long made of polished steel with a very sharp edge and an electronic sensor on the pointed tip. It is held in one hand with a short handle and used to strike an opponent in the sport of fencing.

Badminton shuttle (n) (c) **bad**-min-tn **shuht**-l
This is a small object which is always white. It consists of a **semi-circular** base made of hard plastic and a conical upper section made of feathers attached to a plastic frame. It is hit with a racket in badminton.

Hockey stick (n) (c) **hok**-ee stik
This object is similar in shape to a golf club and is also held by the player while standing and used to hit a small object on the ground. It is used to hit a puck to play hockey or ice hockey.

Study Tip

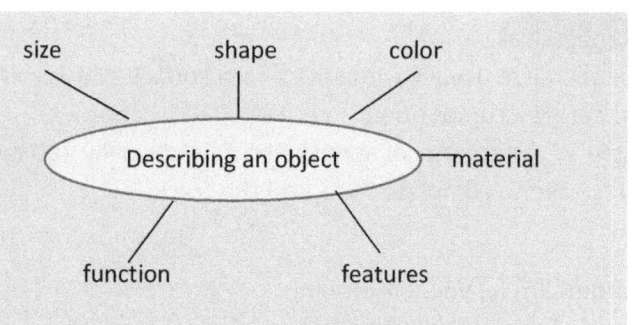

If you do not know the correct name for an object you can describe it and ask your teacher for the correct word. Use the main aspects as shown in the model and the examples on this page. This skill is very useful for learning technical and scientific vocabulary as well as sport vocabulary.

Describing an object: size, shape, color, material, features, function

Section D, Unit 25, Exercises

Exercise 1: Cloze Test

*Fill in the gaps in the following magazine interview with a retired footballer **looking back on** his career. Use the word bank to help you. Number 1 has been done for you.*

> **Word Bank**
>
> marina   referee   *spectate*
> stadium   commentate   velodrome
> pontificate   course   participate

Interviewer: How did you first become interested in football?

Bobby Jones: My dad was an Everton fan, so I went with him to (1) *spectate*.

Interviewer: Did your father play football or just watch.

Bobby Jones: He couldn't play because he had a knee injury from the war. But he always wanted me to (2) …………………………

Interviewer: Was that when you first realized you could play football professionally?

Bobby Jones: Not really. I played a lot of other sports as a kid. I wasn't sure football was my thing.

Interviewer: Tell us about that. What other sports did you do?

Bobby Jones: Cycling for one. I loved it but the equipment was expensive and it was difficult to get to the (3) ……………………….. for races especially after my dad lost his job. Football paid.

Interviewer: So, you signed for Arsenal. Tell us about your best memories of those years? Was it winning the FA Cup?

Bobby Jones: Yeah, definitely. Walking up the steps to get my medal in that huge (4) ………………… at Wembley in front of 100,000 fans. I was only 19 and I still remember the goose bumps.

Interviewer: You had a bit of a reputation as a bad boy; always in trouble with the (5) ………………… and you got sent off a few times, is that right?

Bobby Jones: I made some mistakes. But it meant I had to be careful not to (6) ……………………………. about the officials on TV like some pundits and that made me a better commentator.

Interviewer: Let's move on to your broadcasting career. How did that come about?

Power up your Vocabulary

Bobby Jones: Injury finished me at 27. It was hard to take but I got lucky. An old club colleague was working for the CNN and I was asked to (7) ……………… for them and found I enjoyed it. That gave me a second career.

Interviewer: And now you have retired after, what is it, thirty years behind the microphone do you have time for any other sports?

Bobby Jones: Sure. You'll find me on the golf (8) ……………….. regularly having a round with friends or sometimes at the (9) ………………………. because I am learning yachting from my son in law.

Exercise 2: Complete a Table

Complete the missing words in the following table. Number 1 has been done for you.

Sport	Players/officials	Place	Equipment
squash	referee	court	(1) *racket*
motor racing	(2)	(3)	helmet and overalls
cycling	judges	(4)	racing bicycle
(5)	judges	swimming pool	platform
fencing	fencers	arena	(6)
(7)	players	court	shuttle and racket
hockey	teams	pitch	(8)
cricket	(9)	pitch	bat and ball

Power up your Vocabulary

Exercise 3: Match Suffixes, Compounds and Collocations

Match a word or part of a word from Group A with one from Group B to make words and expressions connected with sport. The first one has been done for you.

		Group A			Group B
1. (j)		athlete's		(a)	club
2. ( )		offici		(b)	stadium
3. ( )		spectat		(c)	ant
4. ( )		yachting		(d)	umpire
5. ( )		rugby		(e)	or
6. ( )		particip		(f)	marina
7. ( )		squash		(g)	racing
8. ( )		horse		(h)	racket
9. ( )		golf		(i)	ate
10. ( )		cricket		(j)	village

Power up your Vocabulary

Section E, Part 1 - Review of the Book

Activity 1: Snakes and Ladders

- *You can play this game with one or more study partners.*
- *Each player needs a colored counter.*
- *Place your counters on square 1.*
- *Shake a dice. The player with the highest number starts.*
- *Throw the dice. If you land on an odd numbered square explain the meaning of the corresponding word in list A below.*

  Example
  You land on square 1, Excavate: *To dig a hole in the ground to find physical remains of the past.*

- *If you land on an even numbered square pronounce and spell the word which is defined in list B below. The first letter is given to help you.*

  Example
  You land on square 2, Two consecutive lines of poetry/verse which rhyme:
  c,o,u,p,l,e,t   *kuhp-lit*

- *You have 30 seconds to complete your answer.*
- *If you are right and you are at the bottom of the ladder go up.*
- *If you wrong and you are on the head of a snake do down.*
- *The winner is the first player to reach square 100.*

List A (odd numbers)

1. *excavate*	3. absurd	5. affect	7. diplomatic	9. precision
11. hemisphere	13. sampling	15. surge	17. flexibility	19. blockchain
21. plagiarize	23. integer	25. get behind	27. canyon	29. trade
31. far-fetched	33. ballet	35. sporadically	37. decimal	39. dissect
41. infer	43. carve	45. regrettably	47. concentration	49. peak
51. inflation	53. illogical	55. technically	57. allegory	59. gradually
61. beta testing	63. enhance	65. broadsheet	67. pesticide	69. spectate
71. circumference	73. hybrid car	75. awareness	77. artifact	79. feat
81. eminent	83. notorious	85. legislate	87. bring down	89. shuttle
91. elegy	93. diversity	95. carbon trading	97. astute	99. disgusting

List B (even numbers)

2. Two consecutive lines of poetry/verse which rhyme. (c…………)
4. Modifies a sentence/passage to consider a topic from a point of view related to money. (f…………)
6. The state of choosing to take actions in order to avert risk or danger. (a…………)
8. Describing two or more events or actions which occur at the same time. There or may not be a cause and effect relationship between them. (s…………)
10. The process of bringing new life to something. (r…………)
12. To make public something which was previously secret. (d…………)
14. Describes the adherents of Karl Marx and his ideas and their influence. (m…………)
16. To improve the quality of something. (e…………)
18. A statement about something which is expected to happen. (p…………)
20. Describing someone who has a powerful, personal quality that impresses others. (c…………)
22. (In sport) An official who awards points based on how well a competitor has performed compared to a set of standards. (j…………)
24. Describing something which is very clean. (s…………)
26. Indicates that you are inferring an assumption an author has made or a conclusion you are drawing from his/her work. (p…………)
28. Describes a period which is believed to set standards of excellence of norms to follow. In Art ancient Greece and Rome, in music the 18th and 19th centuries. (c…………)
30. The skill of being able to do several jobs at the same time. (m…………)
32. To give credit or blame for something to others. (a…………)
34. The differences in lifestyle and opportunities between people who have access to the internet and computer skills and those who do not. (d………… d…………)
36. Describes something which is very large or impressive, better than expected. (s…………)
38. To state that something, usually involving crime or incompetence, is true without evidence. (a…………)
40. Describes something which is easily understood or self-evident. (o…………)
42. A branch of maths which studies angles and triangles. (t…………)
44. A document written by hand on paper or another material, not printed. (m…………)
46. (In business) To analyze data deeply to find hidden patterns in the information. (m…………)
48. Something which stops you from focusing on a task. (d…………)
50. A quantity that can change within the context of a mathematical problem. (v…………)
52. A place, similar to a gas station, where drivers will be able to recharge the batteries of electric cars. (c………… s……………)
54. (In poetry) The rhythmic structure of a verse or set of lines in a poem often involving long and short syllables. (m…………)

Power up your Vocabulary

56. Belief in something which cannot be touched or seen and which cannot be proved or disproved by scientific evidence. (f............)
58. Describes somebody who is obedient and does not argue. (s............)
60. To decrease slightly, usually with the implication that the object will rebound. (d............)
62. (In geometry) A two- dimensional shape with six sides. (h............)
64. To stop increasing or decreasing or do so more slowly. (l............)
66. Material from living things such as straw and tree bark used as fuel to make energy. (b............)
68. (In writing) An introduction which attracts the reader's attention and makes them want to read more. (h............)
70. Describes something which must happen and cannot be avoided. (i............)
72. Software which uses advanced mathematical formulas to make rules which decide which websites or adverts a computer user sees. (a............)
74. The process of liquids turning to gas when heated. (e............)
76. A long-term change in direction. (t............)
78. A large venue, usually circular or oval in shape, with seating for a large crowd of spectators. (s............)
80. An airline which sells cheap tickets but offers few services. (b............)
82. To substitute for somebody e.g. a sick colleague. (f............ i....)
84. A large group of islands of varying sizes which often form a country. (a............)
86. Describes somebody who is always smart and well dressed. (w............ g............)
88. To go before, to come before. (p............)
90. Describes an action which occurs all the time with no breaks. (c............)
92. (in law) Describes a lesser punishment than the maximum allowed or expected by public opinion. (l............)
94. Describing a climate which is very dry with very little rain. (a............)
96. To prove that facts or information are true. (v............)
98. The study of creatures without a backbone. (i............ b............)
100. (in art) The base on which a sculpture stands. (p............)

Power up your Vocabulary

Power up your Vocabulary

Activity 2: Alphabet Quiz

Complete the sentences with words from Units 1-25. The first letter is given to help you. The number in brackets tells you the unit in which the word first appeared. The first one is done for you.

1. A person who is *apathetic* does not have strong views about anything. (6)
2. The Chinese economy has b................... in the last thirty years. (11)
3. C....................... is the quality of showing sympathy towards other people who have suffered misfortune. (24)
4. A d............................ person expects a lot from others and can be difficult to work with. (6)
5. In law e............................. circumstances make a crime less serious. (23)
6. A trend which varies with no clear pattern or direction is said to f.................... (10)
7. In geography a slow moving river of ice is called a g......................... (19)
8. An h............ is a person who inherits money or property after a person's death. (13)
9. To i .... something means to burn it, often use to describe the disposal of waste. (7)
10. To j................... an opinion is to show why it is correct using evidence. (8)
11. K....................... economics includes the theory that governments should intervene in the market during times of economic crisis. (19)
12. A phrasal verb which means to reflect on an event after it has happened l........... .... (9)
13. A person's m............................ is their reason for doing something such as studying or taking up a hobby. (1)
14. In maths the top part of a fraction is called the n .... (15)
15. The adverb o............................ is used to comment on facts which are well known. (12)
16. Celebrities are usually p......................... people who always look good in photographs or on TV. (5)
17. A geometrical figure with four sides is called a q........................ (2)
18. In poetry two words which end with the same sound r.................. (22)
19. A s........................ is a computer program with rows and columns and can do multiple calculations in a single window. (17)
20. A strong adjective often used to describe a horror movie: t............................ (4)
21. The person who officiates at a cricket match is an u......................... (25)
22. The published results of scientific research should always be independently v......................... (8)
23. Bill and Melinda Gates are a very w......................... couple. (5)
24. X
25. Economists use y............................ to measure the performance of an economy. (20)
26. I want to study lions in Africa during my z...................... course at university. (16)

Power up your Vocabulary

Section E, Part 2 - Answers to Exercises
Unit 1

Exercise 1: Word Puzzle

1. experiment	2. registration	3. credibility
4. enrollment	5. dissertation	6. application
7. assignment	8. tenacity	9. commitment
10. communication	11. comprehension	12. motivation
13. classification	14. distraction	15. concentration

Educational campaigner: Malala Yousafzai

Exercise 2: Word Family Table

1. communication, presentation, classification, definition, determination, expectation
2. achievement, improvement
3. comprehension, decision
4. flexibility, credibility, tenacity

in any order.

Exercise 3: Matching

1. permission	2. motivate	3. present
4. distraction	5. application	6. experimental
7. comprehension	8. satisfy	9. satisfactory
10. committed		

Power up your Vocabulary

Unit 2

Exercise 1: Scale

b) hemi c) mono d) bi e) tri
f) quad g) dec h) cent i) multi

Exercise 2: Root Trees

1. universal 2. unification 3. unipolar
4/5 autobiography/ antibiotic (in any order) 6. biodegradable
7. decathlon 8. decimal 9. decimate
10. centenary/centurion (in any order) 12. centigrade

a-1 b-6 c-2 d-5 e-10 f-4 g-11 h-8 i-12 j-7 k-3 l-9

Exercise 3: Word Search (Note: Some of the less obvious words are circled)

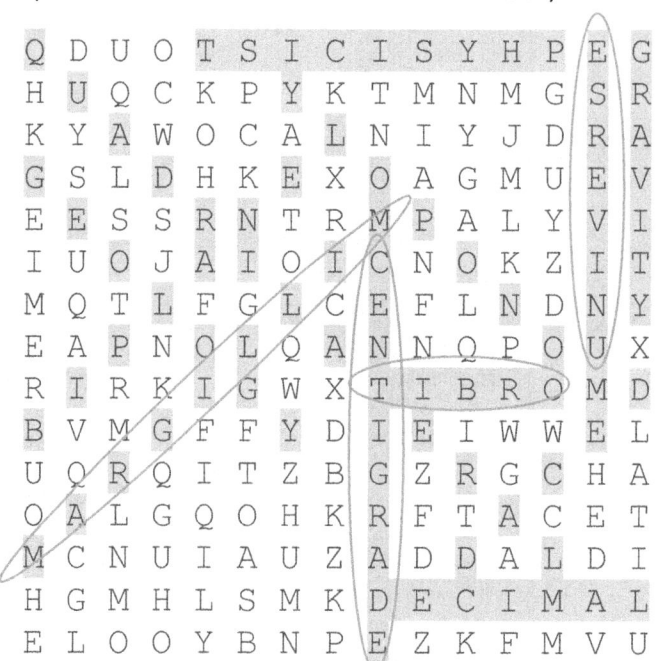

```
Q D U O T S I C I S Y H P E G
H U Q C K P Y K T M N M G S R
K Y A W O C A L N I Y J D R A
G S L D H K E X O A G M U E V
E E S S R N T R M P A L Y V I
I U O J A I O I C N O K Z I T
M Q T L F G L C E F L N D N Y
E A P N O L Q A N N Q P O U X
R I R K I G W X T I B R O M D
B V M G F F Y D I E I W W E L
U Q R Q I T Z B G Z R G C H A
O A L G Q O H K R F T A C E T
M C N U I A U Z A D D A L D I
H G M H L S M K D E C I M A L
E L O O Y B N P E Z K F M V U
```

Power up your Vocabulary

Unit 3

Exercise 1: Compound Crossword

Across 5. hybrid car   6. budget airline   7. carbon footprint   8. renewable energy

Down   1. ozone layer   2. soil erosion   3. charging station   4. eco tourism

Exercise 2: Multiple Choice						
1. d	2. c	3. B	4. d	5. a	6. b

Exercise 3: Word String		
pedestrian zone	greenhouse gas	hybrid car
hydrogen fuel cell	carbon trading	ocean current
ozone layer	eco-tourism	soil erosion

Unit 4

Exercise 1: Ladders

a) hilarious   b) breath-taking   c) disgusting/appalling   d) stupendous

e) astonishing   f) tragic   g) iconic

Exercise 2: Cloze Test

1. terrifying   2. stupendous   3. absurd   4. awful   5. hilarious

6. inspired   7. amazing   8. breath-taking   9. outrageous   10. tragic

Exercise 3: Word Tiles

i) (1+6) disgusting	ii) (3+12) formidable	iii) (5+18) mesmerized	iv) (7+2) dreadful
v) (9+16) thrilling	vi) (11+4) appalled	vii) (13 + 8) iconic	viii) (15 + 10) stupendous
	ix) (17+20) hilarious	x) (19 + 14) breath-taking	

Unit 5

Exercise 1: Matching Synonyms

i) clever/astute
ii) famous/renowned
iii) lively/extrovert
iv) rich/wealthy
v) mass-produced
vi) well-groomed
vii) seductive
viii) designer-label
ix) far-fetched
x) light-hearted

Secret celebrity: Taylor Swift

Exercise 2: Finding Mistakes

1. iconic	2. tenacity	3. wealthy	4. cosmopolitan
5. big headed	6. well-groomed	7. astute	8. notorious
9. level-headed	10. renowned	11. designer-label	12. photogenic

Exercise 3:   Answers will vary.

Unit 6

Exercise 1: Antonym Bingo   Answer: c

a)

probable	serious minded	rational	irrational
illegible	improbable	introvert	passionate
assertive	light hearted	easy-going	blunt
extrovert	irreversible	apathetic	demanding

b)

light-hearted	colorless	passionate	rational
capable	incapable	organized	disorganized
legible	probable	irrational	diplomatic
introvert	submissive	legible	illegible

c) **None**

d)

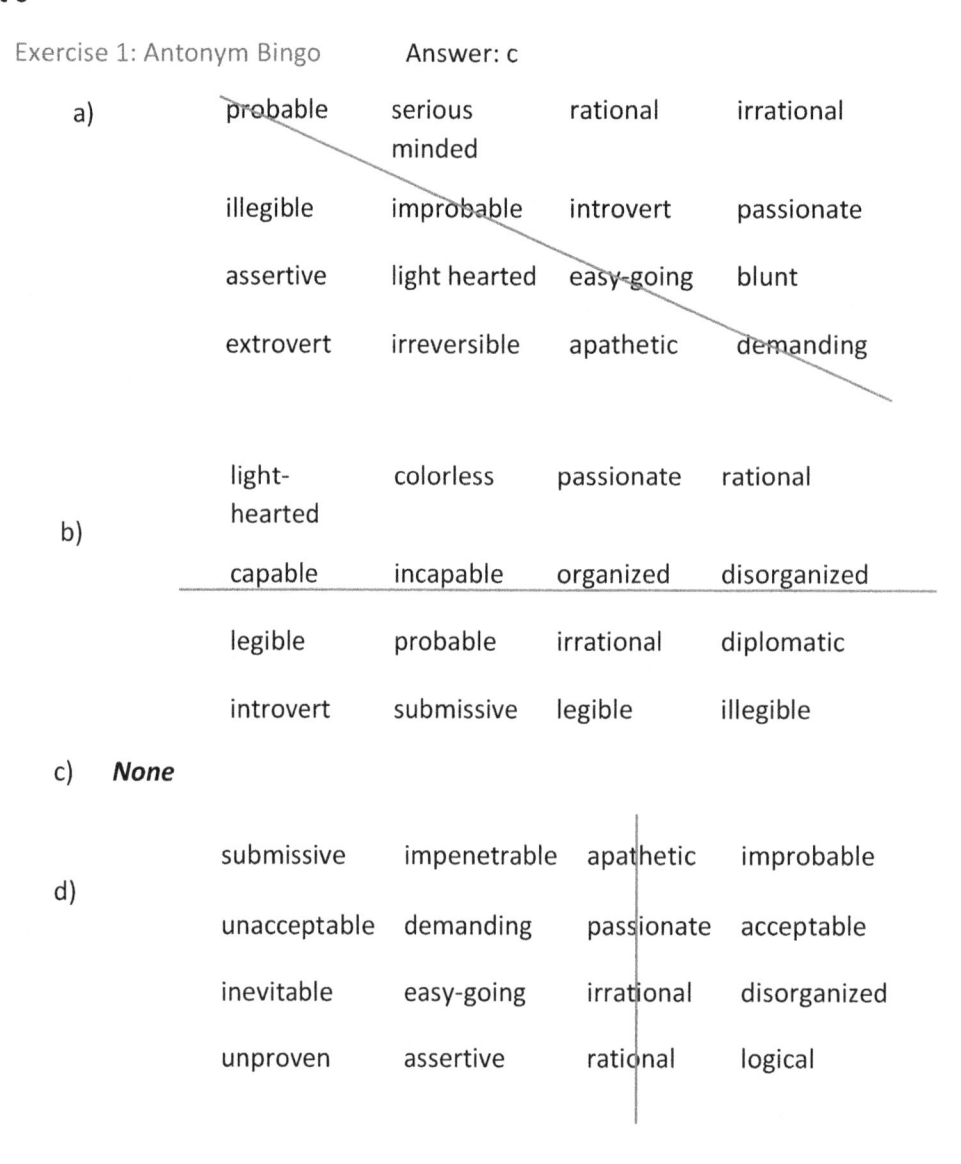

submissive	impenetrable	apathetic	improbable
unacceptable	demanding	passionate	acceptable
inevitable	easy-going	irrational	disorganized
unproven	assertive	rational	logical

Exercise 2: Multiple Choice

1	2	3	4	5	6
c	a	b	c	d	b/d

Exercise 3: Correct the Mistakes. (Suggested answers. There may be other possibilities.)

1. Membership of the WTO is supposed to be irreversible.
2. Examiners prefer (well) organized essays.
3. A serious-minded person is one who rarely laughs.
4. It is improbably/unlikely that there is life on another planet in our solar-system
5. Diplomatic people rarely cause offense.
6. A criminal can only be convicted when the case against him/her is proven.
7. Submissive people obey orders without argument or discussion.
8. A prefix is the beginning of a word.

Unit 7

Exercise 1: Multiple Choice

| 1. b | 2. d | 3. b | 4. a |
| 5. a + d | 6. d | 7. a | 8. c |

Exercise 2: Cloze Test

| 1. engage | 2. experience | 3. mine | 4. transmit |
| 5. advocate | 6. ideas/insights | 7. broadcast | |

Exercise 3: Verb Replacement

2. ~~get~~	generate	3. ~~improve~~	enrich
4. ~~collect~~	harvest	5. ~~make~~	drill
6. ~~pull down~~	demolish	7. ~~put~~	digitize

Unit 8

Exercise 1: Words in the Nest

1. disclosure	2. refutation
3. refutable	4. irrefutable
5. plagiarism	6. implication
7. implicit	8. implicitly
9. verification	10. verified

Exercise 2: Cloze Test

1. assume	2. justify	3. hypothesis
4. correlations	5. inferred	6. announced
7. imply	8. assert	9. refute
10. attribute	11. citation	

Exercise 3: Crossword

Across	Down
4. verify	1. deny
5. dispute	2. reject
6. accusation	3. disclose
7. infer	6. announce
8. assert	

Unit 9

Exercise 1: Memory Game

	2 bring down	3 do away (with)	4 do out (of)
	get down (to)		get out (of)
	break down		look out
	knock down		pull out
5 look up	6 go off	7 go through with	8 look back on
make up (for)		see through	
9 get behind	10 put forward	11 bring round	12 fill in

Exercise 2: Matching Sentence Halves

| a + h | b + f | c + j | d + g | e + i |

Exercise 3: Meanings in Context

1. b   2. b   3. a   4. a   5. b

Unit 10

Exercise 1: Labelling Graphs and Charts (Suggested answers. Other answers may be possible)	
1	Sales fell dramatically then levelled off.
2	Sales fluctuated (throughout the year).
3	Sales peaked (in the middle of the year).
4	Sales of product A rose slightly but those of product B increased sharply.
5	Sales stayed constant (throughout the year).
6	Sales fell sharply at first but then rebounded.

Exercise 2: Cloze Test			
1. significantly	2. constant	3. subsequently	4. climbs
5. dramatically	6. peaks	7. fall	

Exercise 3: Oral Presentation   Answers will vary.

Unit 11

Exercise 1: Word Puzzle			
1. once in a while	2. soar	3. plunge	4. boom
5. generally	6. frequently	7. rocket	
Famous retailer: Walmart			

Exercise 2: Substitution		
1. plummeted	2. soared/rocketed	3. stagnated
4. dip/slip	5. until the cows come home	6. collapse

Exercise 3: Making Sentences   Answers will vary.

Unit 12

Exercise 1: Sentence Completion		
1. apparently	2. obviously	3. respectively
4. frankly	5. chronologically	6. technically
7. presumably	8. fortunately	

Exercise 2: Word Families		
1. specific	2. consequently	3. person
4. apparently	5. financial	6. theory

Exercise 3: Jumbled Syllables		
	Phonic Spelling	English Spelling
1.	uhn-der-**stan**-d*uh*-b*uh* lee	Understandably
2.	**kroo**-sh*uh* lee	Crucially
3.	**def**-*uh*-nit-lee	Definitely
4.	**nawr**-m*uh*-lee	Normally
5.	**tek**-ni-k*uh* lee	Technically
6.	*uh*-**par**-*uh* nt lee	Apparently

Unit 13

Exercise 1: Multiple Choice					
1. c	2. b	3. a	4. d	5. c	6. b

	Exercise 2; Find the Mistakes
1	My French teacher gave me some <u>advice</u> about improving my listening skills.
2	I have applied for an internship and I have an interview with the <u>personnel</u> department next week.
3	My tutor <u>complimented</u> me about the improvement in my maths scores.
4	Jane is my best friend and <u>confidant</u>. I do not know what I would have done without her after my father's accident.
5	If everyone recycles as much of their trash as possible it can have a big <u>effect</u> on the environment.
6	The prisoner was granted <u>bail</u> on condition that he surrendered his passport.
7	The exam question asked "Shakespeare was the greatest English dramatist of all time. To what <u>extent</u> do you agree or disagree with this statement."
8	Prince Charles will be the <u>heir</u> and successor to the present British queen.

Exercise 3: Anagrams		
1. manifest	2. capital	3. spoke
4. allusion	5. proceed	6. compliment

Unit 14

	Hearts = verbs	Diamonds = adverbs	Spades = nouns	Clubs = adjectives
	Suggested answers. Other answers may be possible.			
Ace	travel	chronologically	quadrilateral	...ed
2	rocket soar	extremely really	biplane	fair (pale skin) fair (equal treatment)
3	get behind get down to get on	previously simultaneously subsequently	assignment commitment compliment	il, illegal ir, irresponsible im, impenetrable
4	accuse (v) accusation (n) accuser (n) accusing (adj)	rise fall grow drop	catalytic converter charging station driverless car hybrid car	continuous furious glamorous hilarious
5	Attribute Deny Hypothesize infer imply	apparently frankly personally regrettably unfortunately	tenacity trend trip tripod trigonometry	absent minded big headed level headed light hearted two faced
6	demolish drill enrich excavate generate mine	accusingly definitely dramatically financially frequently technically	application determination elimination investigation motivation registration	astute
7	accuse advise affect assert assume extend look up	chronologically continuously consequently constantly crucially definitely dramatically	Monopoly, Centipede	(far) fetched

8	digitize engage with enhance filter generate livestream mine power up	fortunately legally normally occasionally personally presumably rapidly respectively	manifest	capital charismatic colorless confident cosmopolitan crucially continuously consequently
9	decline decrease fluctuate grow increase peak rise surge soar	generally	classification commitment communication concentration determination expectation flexibility presentation tenacity	extrovert
10	decimate decline decrease demolish deny descend digitize disclose do away with do out of	definitely	decimal	iconic illogical imminent impenetrable improbable inevitable inspired introvert irrational irreversible
Jack	Collocations are words often used together. Example: mine coal.	Comment adverbs are words which express a speaker's or writer's viewpoint in an academic way. Example: fortunately.	Nominalisers are nouns formed by adding a suffix to a verb or an adjective. Example: registration.	Antonyms are pairs of words with opposite meanings. Examples: introvert, extrovert.
Queen	A phrasal verb is a verb + a preposition and/or particle usually with an idiomatic meaning. Example: look back on.	An adverbial is an idiomatic expression which modifies a verb. Example: From time to time.	A suffix is the ending of a word which often tells you the part of speech. Example: ….. sion.	An extreme adjective is at the top or bottom of a scale which cannot be modified with the adverb very. Example: dreadful

Power up your Vocabulary

| King | A word family is made of words representing different parts of speech formed from the same root. Example: motivate (v) motivation (n) motivator (n) motivated (adj.) | An adverb of frequency tells you how often the action of a verb happens. Example: frequently. | A compound noun is a noun + noun structure with a single meaning. Example: hybrid car. | Register is the degree of formality of language. Example: wealthy (formal) loaded (informal) |

Unit 15

Exercise 1: Word Puzzle		
1. integer	2. numerator	3. probability
4. variable	5. formula	6. equilateral
9. polygon	8. median	9. deviation
Mystery Greek mathematician: Pythagoras		

Exercise 2: Complete the Questions		
1. thirty two	2. isosceles	3. mode
4. digit	5. circumference	6. constant
7. correlation coefficient	8. semi-circle	9. binary

Exercise 3: Word Finder   Answers will vary.

Unit 16

Exercise 1: Spidergrams (answers in each spider can be in any order)					
1	decompose	repeatable			
2	eco = house	erg = work	gen = birth	poly = many	
3	zoology	vertebrate biology	invertebrate biology	marine biology	bioengineering	ergonomics
4	objective	prediction	precision	repeatable	anomaly
5	decompose	dissect	distill	ferment	germinate

Exercise 2: Sentence Completion		
1. ferment	2. ergonomics	3. marine biology
4. invertebrate biology	5. Nano technology	6. germinate
A famous Scottish scientist: Alexander Fleming		

Exercise 3: Classification		
Vertebrate biology	c	h
Invertebrate biology	d	f
Marine biology	a	g
Bioengineering	b	e

Unit 17

Exercise 1: Complete the Dialogue			
1. cyber security	2. spreadsheets	3. databases	4. digital divide
5. Internet Service Provider	6. blockchain	7. internet of things	8. algorithms

Exercise 2: Find the IT Phrase			
a) router	b) additive printer	c) network	d) beta testing
e) co-creation	f) knowledge economy	g) cyber espionage	h) connectivity
Place associated with IT: Silicon Valley			

Exercise 3: Word Spiral						
ISP	cloud computing	graphical user interface	cyber espionage	internet of things	CAD/CAM	additive printer

Unit 18

Exercise 1: Multiple Choice definitions and Usage			
1. d	2. b	3. b	4. a
5. b	6. d	7. d	8. c

Exercise 2: Complete a Fact Sheet		
1. regeneration	2. sustainable	3. incidence
4. carbon dating	5. deforestation	6. habitat destruction
7. organic farm	8. sampling	

Exercise 3: Word Search (Note: Some of the less obvious words are circled)

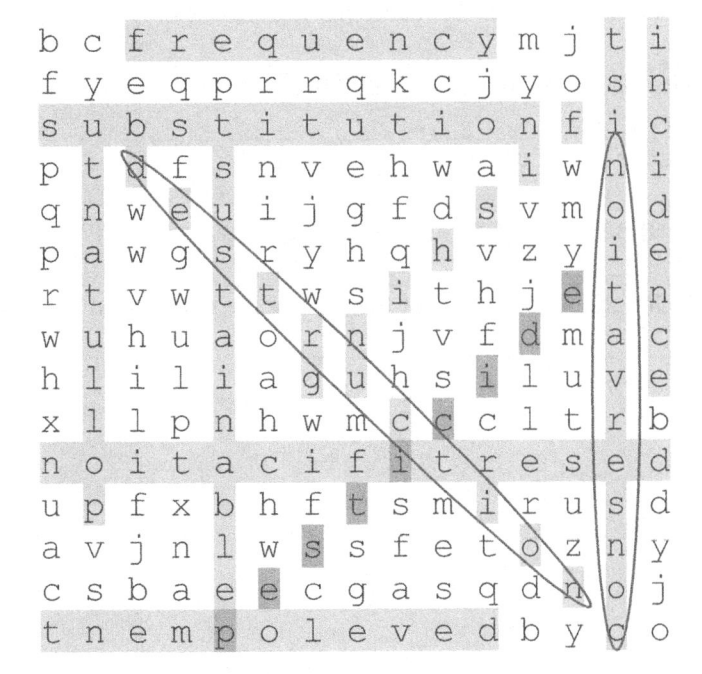

```
b c f r e q u e n c y m j t i
f y e q p r r q k c j y o s n
s u b s t i t u t i o n f i c
p t d f s n v e h w a i w n i
q n w e u i j g f d s v m o d
p a w g s r y h q h v z y i e
r t v w t t w s i t h j e t n
w u h u a o r n j v f d m a c
h l i l i a g u h s i l u v e
x l l p n h w m c c c l t r b
n o i t a c i f i t r e s e d
u p f x b h f t s m i r u s d
a v j n l w s s f e t o z n y
c s b a e e c g a s q d n o j
t n e m p o l e v e d b y g o
```

Unit 19

Exercise 1: Timeline	
1.	Prehistoric
2.	Ancient
3.	Medieval
4.	Renaissance
5.	Post war
6.	Contemporary

Exercise 2: Labelling Pictures	
a)	Canyon
b)	Fjord
c)	Plateau
d)	Glacier
e)	Archipelago

Exercise 3: Correct the Mistakes (Suggested answers, other variations are possible)	
1.	Manuscripts were written by hand before printing was invented.
2.	The north of Canada has an arctic climate.
3.	The adjective equatorial describes something which occurs close to the equator.
4.	If a source is described as biased it means that it presents only one side of an argument.
5.	You can find information about Euclid and Pythagoras in a book about ancient history.
6.	The Sahara Desert is one of the most arid places on earth.
7.	A book entitled "Post War Europe" is about the events after World War II.
8.	In a temperate climate people feel that the weather is neither too hot nor too cold.

Unit 20

Exercise 1: Matching Definitions			
1. g	2. c	3. a	4. f
5. b	6. d	7. e	
The famous economist: John Maynard Keynes			

Exercise 2: Antonyms			
1. deflation	2. full employment	3. surplus	4. macro
5. privatization	6. demand	7. import	

Exercise 3: Describing graphs   Answers will vary.

Unit 21

Exercise 1: Sentence Completion

1. abstract	2. conductor	3. bust
4. impressionist	5. circus	6. carves
7. cubism	8. concerto	

Exercise 2: Anagrams

1. ballet	2. abstract	3. symphony
4. Renaissance	5. visual arts	6. cast
7. marble	8. orchestra	

Exercise 3: Crossword

Across

3. Impressionism	5. sculpture	7. cast	

Down

1. performing arts	2. score	4. opera	6. classical

Unit 22

Exercise 1: Word Search (Note: Some of the less obvious words are circled)

```
C R H R I S T O P T H E R M A
R E L O W E K J S J D H E P Q
E T O U H T P I U K O Y P Y O
K E M R K D T G B M I L U C T
W M R A B A Y C D N J Q R E L
X M U I M A N T A G O N I S T
E V H A T V J O S L W R O J K
R L R W S A U T I N O A Y F Q
K D E X C J S L S R I O M E M
N C J G O L O H B S Z D L Z I
U T U X Y S I G B U C Z G M J
D B F Y M I C M E S I Q U Z V
A N E C D O T E A N N K Q J M
V N M U Z C Z A Q X R H B E L
Q C W X T M Z C V N H E E S W
```

Exercise 2: Multiple Choice							
1. c	2. d	3. b	4. a	5. a + c	6. d	7. a	8. c

Exercise 3: Complete a Table			
1. elegy	2. noun	3. klahy-maks	4. denouement
5. countable	6. rhyme	7. adj	8. theme

Unit 23

Exercise 1: Cloze Test			
1. correspondent	2. sentenced	3. committed	4. investigation
5. enforce	6. incited	7. aggravating	8. draconian

Exercise 2: Matching Definitions			
1. A	2. l	3. c	4. a
5. p	6. o	7. n	8. e
The notorious criminal: Al Capone			

Exercise 3: Suffixes and Parts of Speech		
Group	Words	Part of speech
1 …. tion	allegation, investigation, publication, retraction	noun
2 ….. ian	draconian	adjective
3 …… ing	aggravating, extenuating	adjective
4 …..ive	Investigative, exclusive	adjective
6 ….. ly	rigorously	adverb
7 …. ous	notorious	adjective

Unit 24

	Exercise 1: Correct the Mistakes
1	Multicultural<u>ism</u> is about a society in which people of different cultures live together based on tolerance and respect.
2	Theology is the study of <u>Gods and religions</u> and takes place in universities.
3	Nouns formed with the suffix ….ness are usually uncountable and refer to a <u>state or condition</u>.
4	America is suffering from an epidemic of childhood <u>obesity</u>.
5	Students need to learn strategies for the <u>avoidance</u> of risk when using websites for research.
6	Teachers should show <u>awareness</u> of diversity when preparing lesson plans in schools in **cosmopolitan** cities.

Exercise 2: Independent Writing: Answers will vary.

Exercise 3: Word Puzzle		
1. compassion	2. worship	3. nutrition
4. fitness	5. tolerance	6. consent
7. empathy	8. religion	9. theology
Mystery philosopher: Aristotle		

Unit 25

Exercise 1: Cloze Test		
1. spectate	2. participate	3. velodrome
4. stadium	5. referee	6. pontificate
7. commentate	8. course	9. marina

Exercise 2: Complete a Table		
1. racket	2. clerk of the course	3. track
4. velodrome	5. diving	6. saber
7. badminton	8. (hockey) stick	9. umpire

Exercise 3: Matching				
1. a	2. i	3. e	4. f	5. b
6. c	7. h	8. g	9. a	10. d

Section E: Answers to 'Review of the Book' Exercises

Activity 1: Snakes and Ladders				
Odd numbers: Answers will vary			
Even numbers:			
2. couplet	4. financially	6. avoidance	8. simultaneously
10. regeneration	12. disclose	14. Marxism	16. enhance
18. prediction	20. charismatic	22. judge	24. spotless
26. presumably	28. classical	30. multitasking	32. attribute
34. digital divide	36. stupendous	38. allege	40. obviously
42. trigonometry	44. manuscript	46. mine	48. distraction
50. variable	52. charging station	54. meter	56. faith
58. submissive	60. dip	62. hexagon	64. level off
66. biomass	68. hook	70. inevitable	72. algorithm
74. evaporation	76. trend	78. stadium	80. budget airline
82. fill in	84. archipelago	86. well groomed	88. precede
90. continuously	92. lenient	94. arid	96. verify
98. invertebrate biology	100. plinth		

Activity 2: Alphabet Quiz				
1. apathetic	2. boomed	3. compassion	4. demanding	5. extenuating
6. fluctuate	7. glacier	8. heir	9. incinerate	10. justify
11. Keynesian	12. look back on	13. motivation	14. numerator	15. obviously
16. photogenic	17. quadrilateral	18. rhyme	19. spreadsheet	20 terrifying
21 umpire	22. verified	23. wealthy	24. --------------	25. yardstick
26. zoology				

Section E, Part 3: Alphabetical Word List

A

Absent-minded (adj.) Unit 5 Lesson 2
Abstract (adj.) Unit 21 Lesson 2
Absurd (adj.) Unit 4 Lesson 1
Acid rain (n) (u) Unit 3 Lesson 1
Accuse (v) (T) Unit 8 Lesson 2
Accusation (n) (c) Unit 8 Lesson 2
Accuser (n) (c) Unit 8 Lesson 2
Accusing (adj.) Unit 8 Lesson 2
Accusingly (adv) Unit 8 Lesson 2
Addiction (n) (I) Unit 24 Lesson 1
Additive printer (n) (c) Unit 17 Lesson 1
Advice (n) (u) Unit 13 Lesson 1
Advise (v) (T) Unit 13 Lesson 1
Advocate (v) (T) Unit 7 Lesson 2
Affect (v) (T) Unit 13 Lesson 1
Aggravating (adj.) Unit 23 Lesson 2
Air (n) (u) Unit 13 Lesson 2
Algorithm (n) (c) Unit 17 Lesson 1
Allege (v) Unit 23 Lesson 1
Allegation (n) (c) Unit 23 Lesson 1
Allegory (n) (c) Unit 22 Lesson 1
Allusion (n) (c) Unit 13 Lesson 1
Amazing/amazed (adj.) Unit 4 Lesson 2
Ancient (adj.) Unit 19 Lesson 1
Anecdote (n) (c) Unit 22 Lesson 1
Announce (v) (T) Unit 8 Lesson 1
Anomaly (n) (c) Unit 16 Lesson 2
Antagonist (n) (c) Unit 22 Lesson 2
Apathetic (adj.) Unit 6 Lesson 1
Appalling/appalled (adj.) Unit 4 Lesson 2
Apparently (adv) Unit 12 Lesson 1
Application (n) (c) Unit 1 Lesson 1
Archipelago (n) (c) Unit 19 Lesson 2
Arctic (adj.), (n) (u) Unit 19 Lesson 2
Arid (adj.) Unit 19 Lesson 2
Artifact (n) (c) Unit 19 Lesson 1
Assert (v) (T) Unit 8 Lesson 2
Assignment (n) (c) Unit 1 Lesson 1
Assume (v) (T) Unit 8 Lesson 2
Astonishing/astonished (adj.) Unit 4 Lesson 2

Astute (adj.) Unit 5 Lesson 1
Athlete (n) (c) Unit 25 Lesson 1
Attribute (v) (T) Unit 8 Lesson 2
Avoidance (n) (I) Unit 24 Lesson 2
Awareness (n) (u) Unit 24 Lesson 2

B

Badminton shuttle (n) (c) Unit 25 Lesson 2
Bail (v), (n) (u) Unit 13 Lesson 2
Balance of payments (n) (u) Unit 20 Lesson 2
Bale (n) (c) Unit 13 Lesson 2
Ballet (n) (I) Unit 21 Lesson 1
Beta testing (n) (u) Unit 17 Lesson 2
Biased (adj.) Unit 19 Lesson 1
Big-headed (adj.) Unit 5 Lesson 2
Binary numbers (n) (plural) Unit 15 Lesson 1
Biodegradable (adj.) Unit 2 Lesson 2
Bioengineering (n) (u) Unit 16 Lesson1
Biology (n) (u) Unit 2 Lesson 1
Biomass (n) (u) Unit 2 Lesson 1
Biplane (n) (c) Unit 2 Lesson 2
Blockchain (n) (u) Unit 17 Lesson 1
Blunt (adj.) Unit 6 Lesson 1
Boom (v) (I) Unit 11 Lesson 1
Broadsheet (newspaper) (n) (c) Unit 23 Lesson 1
Break down (v) (T) Unit 9 Lesson 2
Breath-taking (adj.) Unit 4 Lesson 1
Bring down (v) (T) Unit 9 Lesson 1
Bring round (v) (T) Unit 9 Lesson 1
Broadcast (v) (T) Unit 7 Lesson 1
Budget airline (n) (c) Unit 3 Lesson 2
Bust (n) (c) Unit 21 Lesson 2
Byline (n) (c) Unit 23 Lesson 1

C

CAD/CAM (n) (u) Unit 17 Lesson 1
Canyon (n) (c) Unit 19 Lesson 2

Power up your Vocabulary

Capital (adj.), (n) (c) Unit 13 Lesson 2
Capital (n) (u) Unit 20 Lesson 1
Carbon capture (n) (u) Unit 3 Lesson 1
Carbon dating (n) (u) Unit 18 Lesson 2
Carbon footprint (n) (c) Unit 3 Lesson 1
Carbon trading (n) (u) Unit 3 Lesson 1
Carve (v) (T) Unit 21 Lesson 2
Cast (v) (T) Unit 21 Lesson 2
Cast (n) (I) Unit 22 Lesson 2
Catalytic converter (n) (c) Unit 3 Lesson 1
Centenary (n) (c) Unit 2 Lesson 2
Centigrade (n) (c) Unit 2 Lesson 2
Centipede (n) (c) Unit 2 Lesson 2
Centurion (n) (c) Unit 2 Lesson 2
Charging station (n) (c) Unit 3 Lesson 2
Charismatic (adj.) Unit 5 Lesson 1
Chronicle (n) (c) Unit 19 Lesson 1
Chronologically (adv) Unit 12 Lesson 2
Circumference (n) (c) Unit 15 Lesson 2
Circus (n) (I) Unit 21 Lesson 1
Cite (v) Unit 8 Lesson 2
Citation (n) (c) Unit 8 Lesson 2
Classical (adj.) Unit 21 Lesson 2
Classification (n) (I) Unit 1 Lesson 1
Clerk of the course (n) (c) Unit 25 Lesson 1
Climax (n) (c) Unit 22 Lesson 2
Climb (v) (I), (n) (c Unit 10 Lesson 1
Cloud computing (n) (u) Unit 17 Lesson 2
Co-creation (n) (u) Unit 17 Lesson 2
Collapse (v) (I) Unit 11 Lesson 1
Colorless (adj.) Unit 6 Lesson 1
Commentate (v) (T) Unit 25 Lesson 1
Commit (v) (T) Unit 23 Lesson 2
Commitment (n) (c) Unit 1 Lesson 2
Communication (n) (c) Unit 1 Lesson 2
Compassion (n) (u) Unit 24 Lesson 2
Complement (v) (T) Unit 13 Lesson 2
Compliment (v), (n) (c) Unit 13 Lesson 2
Comprehension (n) (u) Unit 1 Lesson 2
Concentration (n) (u) Unit 1 Lesson 2
Concentration (n) (u) Unit 18 Lesson 2
Concerto (n) (c) Unit 21 Lesson 1
Conductor (n (c) Unit 21 Lesson 1
Confidant (n) (c) Unit 13 Lesson 1

Confident (adj.) Unit 13 Lesson 1
Connectivity (n) (u) Unit 17 Lesson 2
Consent (n) (I) Unit 24 Lesson 2
Conservation (n) (u) Unit 18 Lesson 2
Constant (n) (c), (adj.) Unit 15 Lesson 1
Continuously (adv) Unit 11 Lesson 2
Correlate (v) (T) Unit 8 Lesson 1
Correlation coefficient (n) (c) Unit 15 Lesson 2
Correspondent (n) (c) Unit 23 Lesson 1
Consequently (adv) Unit 12 Lesson 2
Constantly (adv) Unit 10 Lesson 2
Couplet (n) (c) Unit 22 Lesson 2
Course (n) (c) Unit 25 Lesson 2
Cosmology (n) (u) Unit 2 Lesson 1
Cosmopolitan (adj.) Unit 5 Lesson 1
Credibility (n) (u) Unit 1 Lesson 2
Crucially (adv) Unit 12 Lesson 2
Cubism (n) (u) Unit 21 Lesson 2
Cubist (adj.), (n) (c) Unit 21 Lesson 2
Cyber-crime (n) (u) Unit 17 Lesson 2
Cyber espionage (n) (c) Unit 17 Lesson 2
Cyber Security (n) (c) Unit 17 Lesson 2

D

Database (n) (c) Unit 17 Lesson 1
Decade (n) (c) Unit 2 Lesson 2
Decathlon (n) (c) Unit 2 Lesson 2
Decimal (adj.) Unit 2 Lesson 2
Decimate (v) Unit 2 Lesson 2
Decline (v) (T) Unit 10 Lesson 1
Decompose (v) (T) Unit 16 Lesson 1
Decrease (v) (T), (n) (c) Unit 10 Lesson 1
Deficit (n) (c) Unit 20 Lesson 2
Definitely (adv) Unit 12 Lesson 1
Deflation (n) (u) Unit 20 Lesson 2
Deforestation (n) (u) Unit 18 Lesson 1
Demand (n) (I) Unit 20 Lesson 1
Demanding (adj.) Unit 6 Lesson 1
Demolish (v) (T) Unit 7 Lesson 1
Denominator (n) (c) Unit 15 Lesson 1
Denouement (n) (c) Unit 22 Lesson 2
Deny (v) (T) Unit 8 Lesson 1
Descend (v) (T) Unit 10 Lesson 1

Power up your Vocabulary

Desertification (n) (u) Unit 18 Lesson 1
Designer-label (adj.) Unit 5 Lesson 2
Dreadful (adj.) Unit 4 Lesson 2
Determination (n) (u) Unit 1 Lesson 2
Digit (n) (c) Unit 15 Lesson 1
Digital divide (n) (u) Unit 17 Lesson 2
Digitize (v) (T) Unit 7 Lesson 2
Dip (v) (T) Unit 11 Lesson 1
Diplomatic (adj.) Unit 6 Lesson 1
Disclose (v) (T) Unit 8 Lesson 1
Discreet (adj.) Unit 13 Lesson 2
Discrete (adj.) Unit 13 Lesson 2
Disgusting/disgusted (adj.) Unit 4 Lesson 2
Disorganized (adj.) Unit 6 Lesson 2
Dissect (v) (T) Unit 16 Lesson 1
Dissertation (n) (c) Unit 1 Lesson 1
Distill (v) (T) Unit 16 Lesson 1
Distraction (n) (u) Unit 1 Lesson 2
Diversity (n) (u) Unit 24 Lesson 1
Do away with (v) (T) Unit 9 Lesson 1
Do out of (v) (T) Unit 9 Lesson 1
Draconian (adj.) Unit 23 Lesson 2
Dramatically (adv) Unit 10 Lesson 2
Drill [for] (v) (T) Unit 7 Lesson 1
Driverless car (n) (c) Unit 3 Lesson 2
Drop (v) (T), (n) (c) Unit 10 Lesson 1
Durable (adj.) Unit 21 Lesson 2

E
Easy-going (adj.) Unit 6 Lesson 1
Economy (n) (I) Unit 20 Lesson 2
Economic (adj.) Unit 20 Lesson 2
Economic growth (n) (u) Unit 20 Lesson 2
Economics (u) (u) Unit 20 Lesson 2
Economist (n) (c) Unit 20 lesson 2
Ecosystem (n) (c) Unit 16 Lesson 2
Eco tourism (n) (u) Unit 3 Lesson 2
Effect (n) (c) Unit 13 Lesson 1
Effluent (n) (I) Unit 18 Lesson 1
Electromagnetism (n) (u) Unit 1 Lesson 1
Elegy (n) (c) Unit 22 Lesson 2
Elimination (n) (I) Unit 1 Lesson 1
Eminent (adj.) Unit 13 Lesson 1

Empathy (n) (u) Unit 24 Lesson 1
Enforce (v) (T) Unit 23 Lesson 2
Engage [with] (v) (T) Unit 7 Lesson 1
Enhance (v) (T) Unit 7 Lesson 2
Enrich (v) (T) Unit 7 Lesson 1
Enrollment (n) (u) Unit 1 Lesson 1
Environmentally (adv) Unit 12 Lesson 2
Epidemic (n) (c) Unit 24 Lesson 1
Equation (n) (c) Unit 15 Lesson 1
Equatorial (adj.) Unit 19 Lesson 2
Equilateral triangle (n) (c) Unit 15 Lesson 2
Ethics (n) (u) Unit 24 Lesson 2
Evaporation (n) (u) Unit 1 lesson 2
Excavate (v) (T) Unit 7 Lesson 1
Exclusive (adj.), (n) (c) Unit 23 Lesson 1
Expectation (n) (c) Unit 1 Lesson 2
Experiment (n) (u) Unit 1 Lesson 1
Export (v) (T) Unit 20 Lesson 1
Exports (n) (plural) Unit 20 Lesson 1
Extend (v) (T) Unit 13 Lesson 1
Extent (n) (u) Unit 13 Lesson 1
Extenuating (adj.) Unit 23 Lesson 2
Extrovert (n) (c) (adj.) Unit 5 Lesson 1

F
Fair (adj.), (n) (c) Unit 13 Lesson 2
Faith (n) (I) Unit 24 Lesson 2
Fall (v) (T), (n) (c) Unit 10 Lesson 1
Far-fetched (adj.) Unit 5 Lesson 2
Fare (n) (c) Unit 13 Lesson 2
Feat (n) (c) Unit 13 Lesson2
Feet (n) (plural) Unit 13 Lesson 2
Ferment (v) (T) Unit 16 Lesson 1
Fill in (v) (T) Unit 9 Lesson 2
Filter [out] (v) (T) Unit 7 Lesson 1
Financially (adv) Unit 12 Lesson 2
Fitness (n) (u) Unit 24 Lesson 1
Fjord (n) (c) Unit 19 Lesson 2
Flexibility (n) (u) Unit 1 Lesson 2
Fluctuate (v) (I) Unit 10 Lesson 2
Formidable (adj.) Unit 4 Lesson 1
Formula (n) (c) Unit 15 Lesson 1
Fortunately (adv) Unit 12 Lesson 1

Power up your Vocabulary

Frankly (adv) Unit 12 Lesson 1
Frequency (n) (I) Unit 18 Lesson 2
Frequently (adv) Unit 11 Lesson 2
From time to time (adverbial) Unit 11 Lesson2
Full employment (n) (u) Unit 20 Lesson 2
Furious (adj.) Unit 4 Lesson 1

G
Generally (adv) Unit 11 Lesson 2
Generate (v) (T) Unit 7 Lesson 1
Genre (n) (c) Unit 22 Lesson 1
Geology (n) (u) Unit 2 Lesson 1
Genetic engineering (n) (u) Unit 16 Lesson 2
Germinate (v) (T) Unit 16 Lesson 1
Get behind (v) (T) Unit 9 Lesson 2
Get down to (v) (T) Unit 9 Lesson 2
Glacier (n) (c) Unit 19 Lesson 2
Glamorous (adj.) Unit 5 Lesson 1
Golf club (n) (c) Unit 25 Lesson 2
Go off (v) (T) Unit 9 Lesson 1
Go through with (v) (T) Unit 9 Lesson 1
Graphical User Interface (n) (c) Unit 17 Lesson 1
Gradually (adv) Unit 10 Lesson 2
Gravity (n) (u) Unit 2 Lesson 1
Greenhouse gas (n) (c) Unit 3 Lesson 1
Gross Domestic Product (GDP) Unit 20 Lesson 2 (n) (u)
Grow (v) (I) Unit 10 Lesson 1

H
Habitat destruction (n) (u) Unit 18 Lesson 1
Harvest (v) (T) Unit 7 Lesson 1
Heavy metal (n) (c) Unit 18 Lesson 1
Heir (n) (c) Unit 13 Lesson 2
Hemisphere (n) (c) Unit 2 Lesson 2
Hilarious (adj.) Unit 4 Lesson 1
Hockey stick (n) (c) Unit 25 Lesson 2
Hook (n) (c) Unit 22 Lesson 1
Hybrid car (n) (c) Unit 3 Lesson 2
Hydrogen Fuel Cell (n) (c) Unit 3 Lesson 2
Hypothesize (v) (T) Unit 8 Lesson 2

I
Iconic (adj.) Unit 4 Lesson 2
Illogical (adj.) Unit 6 Lesson 2
Illusion (n) (c) Unit 13 Lesson 1
Imminent (adj.) Unit 13 Lesson 1
Impenetrable (adj.) Unit 6 Lesson 2
Imply (v) (T) Unit 8 Lesson 2
Import (v) (T) Unit 20 Lesson 1
Imports (n) (plural) Unit 20 Lesson 1
Impressionism (n) (u) Unit 21 Lesson 2
Impressionist adj.), (n) (c) Unit 21 Lesson 2
Improbable (adj.) Unit 6 Lesson 2
Incinerate (v) (T) Unit 7 Lesson 1
Incite (v) (T) Unit 23 Lesson 1
Inclusiveness (n) (u) Unit 24 Lesson 1
Increase (v) (T), (n) (c) Unit 10 Lesson 1
Inevitable (adj.) Unit 6 Lesson 2
Infer (v) (T) Unit 8 Lesson 2
Inflation (n) (u) Unit 20 Lesson 2
Incidence (n) (u) Unit 18 Lesson 2
Inspired (adj.) Unit 4 Lesson 1
Integer (n) (c) Unit 15 Lesson 1
Internet of things (n) (u) Unit 17 Lesson 2
Internet Service Provider (n) (c) Unit 17 Lesson 1
Introvert (n) (c) (adj.) Unit 6 Lesson 1
Invertebrate biology (n) (u) Unit 16 Lesson 1
Investigate (v) Unit 23 Lesson 1
Investigative (adj.) Unit 23 Lesson 1
Investigation (n) (I) Unit 23 Lesson 1
Irrational (adj.) Unit 6 Lesson 2
Irreversible (adj.) Unit 6 Lesson 2
Isosceles triangle (n) (c) Unit 15 Lesson 2

J
Judge (n) (c) Unit 25 Lesson 1
Justify (v) (T) Unit 8 Lesson 2

K
Keynesian (adj.) Unit 20 Lesson 2
Knock down (v) (T) Unit 9 Lesson 2
Knowledge economy (n) (c) Unit 17 Lesson 2

Power up your Vocabulary

L

Labor (n) (u) Unit 20 Lesson 1
Legally (adv) Unit 12 Lesson 2
Legislate (v) (T) Unit 23 Lesson 2
Lenient (adj.) Unit 23 Lesson 2
Level-headed (adj.) Unit 5 Lesson 2
Level off (v) (I) Unit 10 Lesson 2
Light-hearted (adj.) Unit 5 Lesson 2
Literary device (n) (c) Unit 22 Lesson 2
Livestream (v) (T) Unit 7 Lesson 2
Logical (adj.) Unit 6 Lesson 2
Long-haul flight (n) (c) Unit 3 Lesson 2
Look back on (v) (T) Unit 9 Lesson 1
Look into (v) (T) Unit 9 Lesson 1
Look up (v) (T) Unit 9 Lesson 1
Lunar calendar (n) (u) Unit 2 Lesson 1

M

Macroeconomics (n) (u) Unit 20 Lesson 1
Make up for (v) (T) Unit 9 Lesson 1
Manifest (v), (n) (c), (adj.) Unit 13 Lesson 2
Manuscript (n) (c) Unit 19 Lesson 1
Marble (n) (c) Unit 21 Lesson 2
Marina (n) (c) Unit 25 Lesson 2
Marine biology (n) (u) Unit 16 Lesson 1
Marxism (n) (u) Unit 20 Lesson 2
Marxist (adj.) Unit 20 Lesson 2
Mass-produced (adj.) Unit 5 Lesson 2
Mean (n) (c), (adj.) Unit 15 Lesson 2
Median (n) (c) Unit 15 Lesson 2
Medieval (adj.) Unit 19 Lesson 1
Memoirs (n) (plural) Unit 22 Lesson 1
Mesmerizing/mesmerized (adj.) Unit 4 Lesson 2
Meter (n) (I) Unit 22 Lesson 2
Microeconomics (n) (u) Unit 20 Lesson 1
Milligram (n) (c) Unit 2 Lesson 2
Mine (v) (T) Unit 7 Lesson 1
Mode (n) (c) Unit 15 Lesson 2
Monetarism (n) (u) Unit 20 Lesson 2
Monetarist (adj.), (n) (c) Unit 20 Lesson 2
Monopoly (n) (c) Unit 2 Lesson 2

Monorail (n) (I) Unit 3 Lesson 2
Monsoon (adj.), (n) (c) Unit 19 Lesson 2
Most of the time (adverbial) Unit 11 Lesson 2
Motivation (n) (u) Unit 1 Lesson 2
Multiculturalism (n) (u) Unit 24 Lesson 1
Multi-tasking (n) (u) Unit 2 Lesson 2

N

Nano technology (n) (I) Unit 16 Lesson 2
Narrative (n) (c) Unit 22 Lesson 1
Nationalization (n) (u) Unit 20 Lesson 1
Network (n) (c) Unit 17 Lesson 1
Normally (adv) Unit 12 Lesson 1
Notorious (adj.) Unit 5 Lesson 1
Now and again (adverbial) Unit 11 Lesson 2
Numerator (n) (c) Unit 15 Lesson 1
Nutrition (n) (u) Unit 24 Lesson 1

O

Obesity (n) (u) Unit 24 Lesson 1
Objective (n) (c) Unit 16 Lesson 2
Obviously (adv) Unit 12 Lesson 1
Occasionally (adv) Unit 11 Lesson 2
Ocean current (n) (c) Unit 3 Lesson 1
Officiate (v) (T) Unit 25 Lesson 1
Once in a while (adverbial) Unit 11 Lesson 2
Opera (n) (I) Unit 21 Lesson 1
Opponent (n) (c) Unit 13 Lesson 1
Oral history (n) (I) Unit 19 Lesson 1
Orbit (n) (c) Unit 2 Lesson 1
Orchestra (n (c) Unit 21 Lesson 1
Organic farming (n0 (u) Unit 18 Lesson 2
Organized (adj.) Unit 6 Lesson 2
Outrageous (adj.) Unit 4 Lesson 2
Outgoing (adj.) Unit 6 Lesson 1
Over fishing (n) (u) Unit 18 Lesson 1
Ozone layer (n) (u) Unit 3 Lesson 1

Power up your Vocabulary

P

Participate (v) Unit 25 Lesson 1
Particulate Matter (PM) (n) (u) Unit 18 Lesson 1
Passionate (adj.) Unit 6 Lesson 1
Peak (v) (I) Unit 10 Lesson 2
Pedestrian zone (n) (c) Unit 3 Lesson 2
Performing arts (n) (plural) Unit 21 Lesson 1
Personal (adj.) Unit 13 Lesson 1
Personally (adv.) Unit 12 Lesson 2
Personnel (n) (plural) Unit 13 Lesson 1
Pesticide (n) (c) Unit 18 Lesson 1
Photogenic (adj.) Unit 5 Lesson 1
Physicist (n) (c) Unit 2 Lesson 1
Plagiarize (v) (T) Unit 8 Lesson 2
Plagiarized (adj.) Unit 8 Lesson 2
Plagiarizer (n) (c) Unit 8 Lesson 2
Plagiarism (n) (u) Unit 8 Lesson 2
Planet (n) (c) Unit 2 Lesson 1
Playwright (n) (c) Unit 22 Lesson 2
Plateau (n) (c) Unit 19 Lesson 2
Plinth (n) (c) Unit 21 Lesson 2
Plummet (v) (I) Unit 11 Lesson 1
Plunge (v) (T) Unit 11 Lesson 1
Pollutant (n) (c) Unit 18 Lesson 1
Polygon (n) (c) Unit 15 Lesson 2
Polymer (n) (c) Unit 16 Lesson 2
Pontificate (v) Unit 25 Lesson 1
Post war (adj.) Unit 19 Lesson 1
Power-up (v) (T) Unit 7 Lesson 2
Precede (v) (T) Unit 13 Lesson 1
Precision (n) (u) Unit 16 Lesson 2
Prediction (n) (c) Unit 16 Lesson 2
Prehistoric (adj.) Unit 19 Lesson 1
Presentation (n) (c) Unit 1 Lesson 1
Presumably (adv) Unit 12 Lesson 1
Previously (adv) Unit 10 Lesson 2
Privatization (n) (u) Unit 20 Lesson 1
Probable (adj.) Unit 6 Lesson 2
Probability (n) (c) Unit 15 Lesson 1
Proceed (v) (I) Unit 13 Lesson 1
Proponent (n) (c) Unit 13 Lesson 1
Proven (adj.) Unit 6 Lesson 2
Publish (v) Unit 23 Lesson 2
Publication (n) (I) Unit 23 Lesson 2
Pull out (v) (T) Unit 9 Lesson 2
Put forward (v) (T) Unit 9 Lesson 2

Q

Quadrilateral (n) (c) Unit 2 Lesson 2

R

Rapidly (adv) Unit 10 Lesson 2
Rational (adj.) Unit 6 Lesson 2
Raw material (n) (c) Unit 20 Lesson 1
Rebound (v) (I) Unit 10 Lesson 1
Referee (n) (c) Unit 25 Lesson 1
Refute (v) (T) Unit 8 Lesson 2
Regeneration (n) (u) Unit 18 Lesson 2
Registration (n) (u) Unit 1 Lesson 1
Regrettably (adv) Unit 12 Lesson 1
Reject (v) (T) Unit 8 Lesson 1
Religion (n) (c) Unit 24 Lesson 2
Remand (n) (u), (v) Unit 23 Lesson 2
Renaissance (adj.) (n) (u) Unit 21 Lesson 2
Renowned (adj.) Unit 5 Lesson 1
Repeatable (adj.) Unit 16 Lesson 2
Respectively (adv) Unit 12 Lesson 2
Retort (v) (T) Unit 8 Lesson 1
Retract (v) Unit 23 Lesson 1
Rhyme (v), (n) (I) Unit 22 Lesson 2
Ride sharing app (n) (c) Unit 3 Lesson 2
Rigorously (adv.) Unit 23 Lesson 2
Rise (v) (I), (n) (c) Unit 10 Lesson 1
Rocket (v) (I) Unit 11 Lesson 1
Router (n) (c) Unit 17 Lesson 1

S

Saber (n) (c) Unit 25 Lesson 2
Saga (n) (c) Unit 22 Lesson 2
Salinity (n) (u) Unit 18 Lesson 1
Sampling (n) (u) Unit 18 Lesson 2

Satire (n) (c) Unit 22 Lesson 1
Scintillating (adj.) Unit 4 Lesson 1
Score (n) (c) Unit 21 Lesson 1
Sculpture (n) (I) Unit 21 Lesson 2
Sculptor (n) (c) Unit 21 Lesson 2
Sedentary (adj.) Unit 5 Lesson 1
See through (v) (T) Unit 9 Lesson 2
Semicircle (n) (c) Unit 15 Lesson 2
Sentence (n) (I), (v) Unit 23 Lesson 2
Serious-minded (adj.) Unit 6 Lesson 1
Setting (n) (c) Unit 22 Lesson 1
Sharply (adv.) Unit 10 Lesson 2
Significantly (adv.) Unit 10 Lesson 2
Simplify (v) Unit 15 Lesson 1
Simultaneously (adv.) Unit 10 Lesson 2
Slightly (adv.) Unit 10 Lesson 2
Slip (v) (I) Unit 11 Lesson 1
Soar (v) (I) Unit 11 Lesson 1
Soil erosion (n) (u) Unit 3 Lesson 1
Solar power (n) (u) Unit 2 Lesson 1
Soliloquy (n) (c) Unit 22 Lesson 2
Sow (v), (n) (c) Unit 13 Lesson 2
Specifically (adv.) Unit 12 Lesson 2
Spectate (v) (T) Unit 25 Lesson 1
Spirituality (n) (u) Unit 24 Lesson 2
Spoke (v), (n) (c) Unit 13 Lesson 2
Sporadically (adv.) Unit 11 Lesson 2
Spotless (adj.) Unit 4 Lesson 2
Spreadsheet (n) (c) Unit 17 Lesson 1
Squash racket (n) (c) Unit 25 Lesson 2
Stadium (n) (c) Unit 25 Lesson 2
Stagnate (v) (I) Unit 11 Lesson 1
Standard deviation (n) (c) Unit 15 Lesson 2
Stay constant (v) + (n) Unit 10 Lesson 2
Stupendous (adj.) Unit 4 Lesson 1
Submissive (adj.) Unit 6 Lesson 1
Subsequently (adv.) Unit 10 Lesson 2
Substitution (n) (I) Unit 18 Lesson 2
Supply (n) (I) Unit 20 Lesson 1
Surge (v) (I) Unit 11 Lesson 1
Surplus (n) (c) Unit 20 Lesson 2
Sustainable Development (n) (I) Unit 18 Lesson 2
Symphony (n) (c) Unit 21 Lesson 1

T
Tabloid (newspaper) (n) (c) Unit 23 Lesson 1
Technically (adv) Unit 12 Lesson 2
Temperate (adj.) Unit 19 Lesson 2
Tenacity (n) (u) Unit 1 Lesson 1
Terrifying (adj.) Unit 4 Lesson 1
Theme (n) (c) Unit 22 Lesson 1
Theology (n) (u) Unit 24 Lesson 2
Thrilling/thrilled (adj.) Unit 4 Lesson 2
Tolerance (n) (u) Unit 24 Lesson 1
Track (n) (c) Unit 25 Lesson 2
Tragic (adj.) Unit 4 Lesson 1
Trigonometry (n) (u) Unit 2 Lesson 2
Trade (n) (I) Unit 20 Lesson 1
Transmit (v) (T) Unit 7 Lesson 2
Travel (v) (I) Unit 13 Lesson 1
Trend (n) (c), (v) Unit 10 Lesson 1
Trip (n) (c) Unit 13 Lesson 1
Tripod (n) (c) Unit 2 Lesson 2
Two-faced (adj.) Unit 5 Lesson 2

U
Umpire (n) (c) Unit 25 Lesson 1
Unacceptable (adj.) Unit 6 Lesson 2
Understandably (adv) Unit 12 Lesson 1
Unemployment (n) (u) Unit 20 Lesson 2
Unicorn (n) (c) Unit 1 Lesson 2
Unilateral action (n) (I) Unit 2 Lesson 2
Unipolar (adj.) Unit 2 Lesson 2
Unverifiable (adj.) Unit 8 Lesson 2
Universal (adj.) Unit 2 Lesson 1
Unproven (adj.) Unit 6 Lesson 2

V
Variable (n) (c) Unit 15 Lesson 1
Velodrome (n) (c) Unit 25 Lesson 2
Verifiable (adj.) Unit 8 Lesson 2
Verifiably (adv) Unit 8 Lesson 2
Verify (v) (T) Unit 8 Lesson 2
Verification (n) (u) Unit 8 Lesson 2
Vertebrate biology (n) (u) Unit 16 Lesson 1
Visual arts (n) (plural) Unit 21 Lesson 1

Power up your Vocabulary

W
Wealthy (adj.) Unit 5 Lesson 1
Well-groomed (adj.) Unit 5 Lesson 2
Well-heeled (adj.) Unit 5 Lesson 2
When the cows come home (adverbial) Unit 11 Lesson 2
Worship (n) (u) Unit 24 Lesson 2

Y
Yardstick (n) (c) Unit 20 Lesson 2
Yachting (n) (u) Unit 25 Lesson 2

Z
Zoology (n) (u) Unit 16 Lesson 2

Power up your Vocabulary

Additional Bonus Material

We hope that you enjoyed learning from this book and look forward to your feedback.

We would like to provide you with the following additional Bonus Material.

Winners' Guide to English Usage

Correct English usage is critical, not only for Writing , but also for reading.

In this 50 page Guide you will find typical examples of wrong usage by students, and how to avoid them.

TurboCharge your memory

Learn how to memorize information you are taught in class. Multiple examples to teach you material you need for school including vocabulary, foreign languages, mathematics and more….

Learning to Use Your Mind by HARDY KITSON, PH.D.

You will find this book invaluable not only for your school but also college and further studies.

Among other things in this seventy page book, you will learn about:

- *Formation of Study Habits*
- *Brain activity during study*
- *Aids to memory*
- *How to retain attention over long periods*
- *How to become interested in a subject*

……… and much more.

Please send us an email at:

expresseducationlimited@gmail.com

Providing some feedback on how you found the book.

The free gifts will be with you within 5 days of receiving your feedback.